Living, Loving Iran
A Memoir

Living, Loving Iran
A Memoir

James F. Goode

Since 1980
Mazda Publishers
Costa Mesa, California
2021

Publication of this book was made possible by a grant from
A. K. Jabbari Trust

Mazda Publishers, Inc.
Academic publishers since 1980
P.O. Box 2603, Costa Mesa, California 92628 U.S.A.
www.mazdapublishers.com
A. K. Jabbari, Publisher

Library of Congress Control Number: 2021942384

ISBN 10: 978-156859-361-9
ISBN 13: 978-1-56859-361-6
Softcover, alk. paper

Cover photo: Bridge in Oshtorawn.
Back cover photo: Pot maker in Tuyserkan.

To the Ehsani family for their friendship
and support when it mattered most

CONTENTS

Acknowledgments

I would like to thank several Iranian and American friends who kindly read parts of the manuscript and gave me important feedback. These included, Barbara (Johnson) Auerbach, Bahman Farmanara, Tom Gordon, Farhad Kadkhodazadeh, John Limbert, George McDonald, Esmaeil Momtaz, and Hadi Navid. Longtime friends, Sally Chaffee and Nasrin Rahimieh, agreed to read the entire memoir and provided useful comments. Our sons, Matthew and Zachary, also read the entire manuscript, and we discussed, from a distance, their thoughtful and encouraging observations. Zachary also volunteered to help prepare the images for the book. Finally, Virginia, my constant companion since 1972, cheerfully engaged in numerous conversations as the writing progressed. I could ask for no better counsel.

Preface

Iran has filled a large part of my adult life. I first came to know the Iranian people and their culture as a young Peace Corps volunteer, with no clear idea of what the future might hold. I embraced the new world of my small, isolated mountain town, Tuyserkan, and the community reciprocated. As I was drawn into daily life, I lost sight of any larger picture, and focused instead on day-to-day activities, teaching, meeting and socializing with friends, running a household. There were of course difficult times, but the good ones outweighed the bad. It rarely occurred to me how much of an impact these experiences were making on my attitudes toward life. I was gaining greatly in confidence and maturity, but I only came to understand that much later. After three years, I left the Tuyserkan valley a much-changed individual.

I met my first love, also, in Iran. We courted and married in the shadow of Mount Damavand. It all happened so quickly, no long-term engagement for us, barely six months from first date to wedding vows. Together we shared wonderful experiences in a country we both loved. Memories of those early years living in Mashhad remain as vivid as yesterday.

Even after our traumatic exodus, Iran continued to hold sway over my future. I began to study the country in a different way, as an academic, benefitting, of course, from the personal experience of having lived for such a long time among its kind people and of having traveled from one end of the country to the other. Equally important I could access the writings of Iranian political leaders, journalists, and historians in their own language.

Unfortunately, parallel to my scholarly association with Iran, came the steady and long-lasting decline in relations between my country of birth and the country that allowed me to blossom. This is not the place to revisit all the reasons for this distancing, except to admit that the estrangement has caused much personal sorrow.

Over the past four decades, I have responded to the persistent demonizing of Iran through talks, workshops, and writings, working steadily to lift the veil, at least slightly, so that fellow Americans might see a glimmer of the Iran I was privileged to know. In that way they might come to look upon this faraway land with a bit more understanding and kindness. I hope I have achieved some small measure of success in that endeavor.

This memoir continues that project. Here, I invite readers to share the experiences that made such a lasting impact on both of us. Let them judge for themselves the appropriateness of our affection for that distant land.

List of Illustrations

Chapter 1

Peace Corps Group 19 departing for Iran, June 1968 (back row 1st on right, Jim and Mary King, Author, 6th from right. Jim Belcher, 2nd row, 3rd from left)

Winding mountain road into Tuyserkan valley

Hajji (far left) with his family in front of Hotel Alvand

Ehsani children, (l. to r.) Masoud, Saeed and their cousin, Minoo, playing in stream at Gazandar Bala

Turon making lunch in kitchen of my first house, 1969

Doshanbe and Abibi Ehsani

Ehsani, Mahvash and the children in the gardens above Tuyserkan.

Director of Education for Hamadan province (2nd from right) visits my classroom

Mr. Alghaws with his buffalo at his village of Goegtapeh, summer 1969

Seyed and his brother, my nextdoor neighbors, shoveling snow off their flat roof, 1969

Main square in Tuyserkan, winter, 1969

Ehsani, Bashiri, Daboghi (l. to r.) at a gathering at my house, 1969

Hassan Rahmani dancing in a circle of friends at my house, 1968. Mansur and Mashollah Ehsani on left

Prologue

As I approached retirement from Grand Valley State University after thirty-two years of teaching, my wife and I wished to celebrate our departure with an exhibition, emphasizing our intimate connection with the Middle East and especially Iran over the previous fifty years, 1967-2017. Museum Director Henry Matthews, who usually dealt with grander materials, saw immediately, much to his credit, what we intended in the suggested exhibition. After viewing a sample of our collection, he accepted our offer and became quite excited about selecting and preparing items for the gallery. We quickly discovered, however, that bringing our original idea to fruition would take considerable time. Such an exhibition could not happen overnight. This initial step took place in summer 2015, more than two years prior to opening night.

We gathered the artifacts we had acquired over five decades for the perusal of the staff of the university museum and art gallery. Our collecting had taken place more by happenstance than by design; we acquired pieces here and there as we traveled the region. Gradually, the number swelled. We could associate each piece with a particular journey. These were mainly humble items of daily use, for our theme in collecting, if there had been one, was to look for functional items that were in common use across the region. These were traditional pieces that anyone familiar with the cultures of Southwest Asia and the Middle East (Iran, Afghanistan, Egypt, Turkey, Palestine, Morocco, Jordan, Syria, or Lebanon) would immediately recognize. We found that removing these items, clay water jugs, handmade locks, metal trays, sturdy hand-woven carpets, and carpet-making tools, and so forth, from their daily environments, allowed us to examine them at leisure and to focus on their simple and beautiful construction. Then, too, many of these traditional items were rapidly disappearing as the pace of modernization quickened, and alternatives such as plastics, carpet-weaving machines, and refrigerators, took their places.

For us, the exhibition would fulfill a number of important objectives. It would showcase a region of the world—especially Iran—in which we had lived and worked for long periods and studied continuously for most of our adult lives. It was a way of saying thank you to the university community and the general public, who had supported our work since 1986. It would provide a focus for educating students about the cultures of the region, for we planned informal talks on various aspects of Iranian culture, drawing on our shared experiences, throughout the five weeks that the exhibition would remain open.

Having been assigned a date for fall 2017, we set about fleshing out the history of the items that would appear in the exhibition. We actually made several discoveries in this process. In one case, we learned that a painting purchased in the Tehran bazaar in 1970, for example, was the early work of a well-known Iranian-American artist, who had immigrated to the American Southwest shortly after painting this portrait of an old man.

As we worked through the materials, we also took time to revisit episodes of our own half-century of involvement with Iran and the Middle East. How was it that an Aussie and a Yank had come together in that far-off land, a land that had attracted each separately? This seemed a story worth telling. But just as important as what it said about us, was what it revealed about the people of Iran and their culture. This would surely surprise most American readers.

Peace Corps Days, 1968-1971

Setting A Course

My introduction to Iran came through Peace Corps service. As a teenager, I had rooted for John F. Kennedy and the programs of the New Frontier, especially the Peace Corps. He and I had deep ties to Cape Cod, and we even shared a common birthday, May 29. We came from vastly different social backgrounds, of course, I from a working-class family in Hyannis, he from the neighboring elite enclave of Hyannisport. When the Kennedys were in town, we attended the same church—St. Francis Xavier on South Street. The pews up front were reserved for their family members; we selected from the remainder. None of this disparity in wealth or class mattered much to me at the time for I believed that, like FDR, Kennedy understood the problems of the less well off, even though he had never experienced them himself. Then, of course, there was a sense of pride, when a "local" boy—and a Catholic at that—became the presidential candidate of the Democratic Party in 1960. As his campaign developed, the Cape became flooded with journalists and television crews. My father, who drove taxi in Hyannis, regaled us with stories about the media types he would chauffeur around town. Occasionally, he even got a fare to the Kennedy compound or to near-by Squaw Island, where other Kennedys had summer homes. This was all heady stuff for a kid like me, growing up in a small, rural town of coastal Massachusetts.

At the time of the election in November 1960, I was sixteen years old. Although I could not vote, I had followed every detail of the campaign. How exciting to watch my hero go from strength to strength. Strangely, I cannot recall anyone who was not a Kennedy supporter, and yet Richard Nixon carried our county, Barnstable, by a landslide in the election. I must have moved in a narrow circle. In any case, on election night I camped out with several friends in front of the National Guard Armory on South Street in Hyannis. This was where JFK would make his acceptance speech or—heaven forbid—his concession speech once the tight contest had been decided. All through that sleepless night we waited for the final results. It became clear in the wee hours of the morning that the winner would not be known for many more hours. I decided to stay and miss school the next day. I was glad I did. Late in the morning of November 9, Kennedy, now president-elect, arrived at the armory to give a brief acceptance speech. I was ecstatic and exhausted.

In September 1962, I followed JFK to Washington, where I enrolled as a freshman at Georgetown University's School of Foreign Service. As long as I can remember, I had taken great interest in international affairs, following events abroad with much attention. I cannot account for this interest, which was not common among my friends. From an early age, my father, who had himself rarely traveled beyond the Cape Cod Canal, would relate colorful stories of popular history, about the brave Turkish soldiers of World War I at Gallipoli, for example, and I listened intently. He had the Irish gift of gab; he was a fine storyteller. How he acquired an interest in such unusual foreign subjects I never knew. Also, I read a great deal in those early years, and much of that reading focused on popular histories of European wars. Historical fiction also became a favorite genre, especially accounts of imperial wars along the frontier of the British colonies in North America.

When I was a junior in high school, I became close friends with Christine Owocki, a senior, whose family had just arrived in town after living for several years in Zaragosa, Spain, where her father had been stationed with the United States Air Force. She seemed very sophisticated, having lived in such an exotic location, a place I could only dream about. Christine was headed for the Georgetown University Institute of Languages and Linguistics, which shared a campus with the Foreign Service School. I think she must have turned my head in the direction of the Jesuit university. To my high school counselor, "Doc" Levinson, this seemed a quixotic and unwise choice, especially as I was the first in my family to go to college. He tried to persuade me to attend the University of Massachusetts Amherst (UMass) and then with my undergraduate degree in hand, I could consider doing graduate work at Georgetown. But, no, I had made up my mind and nothing could dissuade me, even the fact that I would likely have to pay all the expenses myself. I could be determined—some might say stubborn—a characteristic that has not faded. So here I was at the beginning of the academic year, 1962, setting off for a campus I had never visited. I had flown to Washington once in 1959 with a friend, and we spent ten days taking in all the sights, but Georgetown University had not been one of them.

My friend, Christine, had come to the District of Columbia a year earlier, and she had been filling my head with tales of the wonderful experiences she was having at the university. But I was like a fish out of water. Today, colleges and universities devote a lot of resources toward assisting students from families in which no one has previously attended college, but in the early 1960s, Georgetown, like other tertiary institutions, had no such support. I tried to make the most of it.

One of the first steps I took to fit in was to sign up for Reserve Officers' Training Corps (ROTC). I was an unlikely candidate, being rather pudgy. I had never pictured myself in any uniform other than that of the Boy Scouts. Nor did I come from a military family. Neither my father nor any of my uncles had served in the Second World War, although my older brother had recently entered the United States Coast Guard. So, what was the attraction? In part it was the money, which I would begin to receive in my third year in the corps if I were accepted into advanced training. Also, one of my roommates and several other new acquaintances had signed up, so I went along. The corps in those years was quite large. I had not seriously considered the possible long-term consequences.

I struggled to get out of bed at sunrise for the weekly corps parades and inspections. Taking apart an M-1 rifle and reassembling it—with no parts left over—always proved a challenge. When we were being timed, I sometimes jammed my finger in the powerful spring mechanism. How many fingernails, I wonder, did I lose during those two years? Worst of all, I think, were the endless minutes spent polishing and re-polishing my army issue boots, so that I could see my face in the toes.

At the end of two years, I came up for review. I appeared in uniform before a panel of three army personnel, two officers and a sergeant as I recall. During the interview, the decidedly overweight sergeant asked me what I intended to do about my weight problem. I stammered some feeble response about trying hard in future to lose weight. All the while thinking, "What are you going to do about yours!" My lack of commitment must have appeared obvious to the panel for they rejected me. There would be no monthly checks, and my self-esteem suffered a heavy blow.

As time went on, however, and the United States involvement in Vietnam deepened—as did the demand for second lieutenants—I realized that my rejection had worked for the best. I just wished I had taken a more pro-active stance rather than being so diffident about the whole review process: "if they accept me okay, if they don't that's okay, too."

Vietnam became the constant topic of discussion on campus, especially after LBJ's decision to increase dramatically the American commitment in Southeast Asia. By 1965, I had become convinced that the war was wrong and probably unwinnable, and I wanted no part of it. The few times I saw my brother in those years, we ended up arguing interminably about the war. He favored the strongest measures against North Vietnam.

Fate intervened again in spring 1966, when I received a notice from my local draft board to appear for a physical in Boston on such-and-such a date, which happened to coincide with my graduation day at Georgetown. My father took it upon himself to confront the WWI-veteran who headed the local draft board, at his front door, telling him that it was impossible for me to take the physical because I would be graduating that day in Washington. When my dad told me what he had done, I feared the worst, that he had guaranteed my immediate induction. Instead, I received a follow-up notice, saying the board would issue me another call later in the summer. That second letter never came. By the end of summer, I had received another deferment. I was finally on my way to UMass Amherst, this time to study for an MA degree in history. My own experience illustrated something of the fickleness and unfairness of the draft system in those years before Selective Service adopted the lottery system.

At UMass I found kindred spirits and an environment where I thrived. Opposition to the war became even more intense, with frequent anti-war protests. I became friends with some fellow students, who had gone through the ROTC program and would soon be shipping out to Vietnam. They opposed the war, but ultimately decided to honor their commitments. I sympathized with their predicament.

As for me, I had never lost sight of the promise of the Peace Corps, even though my hero who proposed it had died so tragically in November 1963. It made such good sense to me. I wanted to work abroad, to help however I could, to express my country's concern for the welfare of people in the developing world. More was to be gained from this kind of peaceful sharing of skills, I believed, than from the barrel of an M-16. Furthermore, I had never traveled overseas. I needed that experience in order to settle on a future career path. And so, in summer 1967, I applied and was accepted. In due course, I received another deferment.

I was offered a posting in West Africa, which I declined. I had studied French for five years, and I hoped to be sent to a French-speaking country. In those days, an applicant could decline the first offer, but declining a second would likely end all hope of Peace Corps service. I took a chance. I did not get assigned to a French-speaking nation, instead I drew Iran.

I knew next to nothing about that distant land. The shah still received glowing media coverage in the United States, and I accepted the common view that Mohammad Reza Pahlavi (1941-1979) worked selflessly to modernize his country and uplift his people. Up to that point, I had met only one Iranian, and that was at Georgetown. Sadegh had dated a friend of mine, and I chatted with him a few times at parties. He was older than me and certainly more mature. He expressed very firm ideas about international relations. He was the first person whom I had ever heard criticize the international role of the United States. Rather naively, I assumed that the United States always did good in the world. He especially challenged the American role in his own country and explained how wrong it was for the United States to feed the military ambitions of the shah. I would become utterly frustrated in these exchanges; I tried to refute his charges, but I just did not know enough. After a brief period, he stopped coming to the parties. I never saw him again, but he had made an impact. I began to question American foreign policy more.

Our Peace Corps training program would begin on April 27, 1968, at the Experiment in International Living in Brattleboro, Vermont. In those early years, half of the training still took place in the United States and half in the host country. We were Iran Group 19, designated as TEFL teachers. Thirty-nine would-be volunteers had been invited to training, nine couples, seventeen single men and four single women.

I completed my MA degree in December, so I was able to spend several months at home, working as a substitute teacher. Political events were unfolding rapidly. That winter saw the drama of the TET offensive followed closely by LBJ's decision not to seek reelection. Then in the spring came the assassinations of Martin Luther King, Jr., and Robert Kennedy. All these events made me anxious for action, impatient to get my training underway. Unbeknownst to me, that long stay would be my last on Cape Cod.

Despite my initial eagerness to start the training program, I arrived in Brattleboro with considerable anxiety. I had little personal confidence in those years, and whenever I embarked on a new venture, I struggled to control my nervousness. I had to force myself not to surrender to all the doubts that flooded over me. I was an innocent in spite of my six years in Washington and Amherst. When I read through the biographical information of my fellow trainees, this became—to me at least—readily apparent. They had all engaged in more meaningful activities, or so I thought. One had worked for the U.S. Forest Service, another as a social worker with emotionally disturbed children, a third with a state migrant program. Many more had traveled extensively in Europe and Asia. I listed my interests as coin collecting and gardening.

We trained hard for eight weeks. We were exposed to High Intensity Language Training (HILT), and we seemed to be studying Persian around the clock. Our teachers had been flown in from Iran, and they were incredibly supportive. We naturally became close to them. They encouraged us to use the target language as much as possible and especially at mealtimes. We memorized couplets of Persian poetry—some of which I still recite fifty years later—and engaged in short dialogues with our staff and fellow trainees. We did just about all one could outside Iran to learn this new language. Along with language training, we had lectures on the history and culture of Iran. I can recall nothing that questioned the policies of the shah or his government.

I still remember one remarkable exercise in which we were obliged to take part. Each of us was given a one-dollar bill, and then we were taken by vans out into the rural Vermont countryside and dropped off one by one in isolated settings. The goal was for us somehow to survive until we would be picked up the following day. We could use the dollar, if absolutely necessary, for a phone call to the Peace Corps office to rescue us. It was a scary yet valuable experience, simulating, I think, finding oneself in a strange culture and having to draw on inner resources to survive. Most of us who did not make the phone call came back with amazing stories. One young woman had knocked on the door of a mobile home, and when she told her story the family welcomed her in. She spent the night sleeping in a big bed with several young children. I ended in more favorable surroundings. Dropped at a rural crossroads, I initially felt shocked. What was I going to do? I had never found myself in such a threatening situation. I looked around and saw a pub-restaurant, one of the few buildings in sight. I went in and bought a beer with my dollar and began a conversation with the bartender. He and his wife, a young couple, were from New York City, and they had just opened this renovated building to the public. I had a good deal of restaurant experience, so we had a lot to talk about. It was Saturday night and business was brisk. I washed dishes all evening. After closing, we shared a fine meal, and I slept in one of their comfortable beds. Early the next afternoon, the Peace Corps van retrieved me as planned. I often think back to that experience; it left such a strong impression. I came back to Brattleboro more firmly convinced that I might actually be able to cope on my own in a strange environment.

I doubt that such an exercise could be repeated today. But why, I wonder? Have conditions changed so radically over the last half-century? Or, perhaps, even in 1968, this was a risky exercise that the training staff had devised.

Many foreign students were studying English at SIT during our eight-week stay. One night as we were walking back to our dorm, a group of German students came up behind us, and one of them called out loudly in English, "Cultural Imperialists!" At first, I had no idea what he was talking about. Only later when we were discussing the incident among ourselves did I begin to understand the nature of the insult he had hurled at us. I had never thought of myself as a cultural imperialist, but inevitably that is what I would become. I was expected to introduce American ways of teaching, with the presumption that they were superior to local methods.

At the end of the program on June 23, a letter was placed in each of our mailboxes. Those who had been accepted to continue to Iran were instructed to meet in a particular location. Those few who were rejected were assigned a different meeting place; I never saw any of them again. We were congratulated and given several days leave before we had to reassemble in New York City for the Pan American flight to Tehran.

I do not remember much about those last few days at home. The country was still reeling from the King and Kennedy assassinations, and these horrible events were on everyone's mind. I did a last-minute check to make sure I had all the necessities for my life in Iran. I had bonded well with a number of fellow trainees, so I felt much more relaxed as we approached the second half of our training.

Welcome to Iran

When we gathered at JFK, a Pan Am photographer took a group picture, copies of which the airline later presented to each of us. There were twenty-five of us about to board for the long flight to Tehran. A few others would join us later. We stopped briefly in Rome and then again in Beirut, where we changed planes. That coastal city provided my introduction to the Middle East, balmy breezes off the Mediterranean Sea under a hot sun and cloudless sky. I felt quite important, as I recall. International travel was much less common than today, and still somewhat magical.

As we flew into Iranian airspace, I could see far below us a stark, brown landscape, patches of green here and there and row after row of mountains. To someone from verdant New England, it looked like a barren landscape. Tehran at almost four thousand feet above sea level sat in a bowl partially surrounded by mountains of the Elburz range. Snow-capped Mount Damavand at more than eighteen-thousand feet could be clearly seen to the north as we came into land at Mehrabad Airport on the afternoon of Friday, June 28. I felt excited, yet also apprehensive. Groups of Iranians lined the boulevard leading from the terminal into the city; I thought they had all come out to welcome us to their country. A staff member quickly reminded us that this was the one-day Iranian weekend, and the families I saw were picnicking in the narrow strips of grass along the roadway.

Already a city of more than three million people, Tehran was by far the most important urban center in the country. It towered over all the others. Among the inhabitants of the larger cities, there was constant competition as to which center was better than the others. They compared climate, food, character of the people, purity of the language, beauty of the surroundings. Those other cities, Isfahan, Shiraz, Mashhad, Tabriz, might be more beautiful and historically and culturally more important, but they could not compete with the capital for power, influence, and employment. Thus, it served as a magnet for a steady stream of Iranians from the provinces. Many former peasants came to reside in makeshift accommodations in the southern suburbs.

We stayed at the Polaris Hotel just off bustling Takht-e Jam-shid Avenue, a central location. Once you exited the hotel, it was only a short walk to the Peace Corps offices, which occupied an old, multi-story home set well back from the busy roadway, within its own walled enclosure. Turning in the opposite direction would quickly bring you to the large, walled compound of the US embassy, which would become so well-known during the hostage crisis of 1979-1981.We remained only a few days in the sprawling capital, just long enough to get over the jet lag and complete some necessary paperwork. That was long enough for one of our number to decide he had made a terrible mistake. He was on the next flight back to the States. His leaving surprised and saddened me as well, for he had been a friend during training. I never heard from him again.

Our final destination was the provincial city of Hamadan, where we would complete our training. It lay six hours by bus to the southwest. Much smaller than Tehran, it had a population well below two hundred thousand. Hamadan, ancient Ecbatana, is said to be the oldest continuously lived in city in the world, but most ancient structures lay buried beneath successive layers of occupation. A stone lion, *Sang-e Shir*, thought to be part of the ancient city's gate, sat neglected on a hilltop. One day this monument would become singularly important to all my future plans.

Six major boulevards radiated from the central *meydan* of the city. In the middle of this circle stood an equestrian statue of Reza Shah, father of the then-current ruler. Humble buildings surrounded the area, none more than four stories high. I happened to be in Hamadan once when the shah was visiting, and this whole central area was transformed. Banners had been raised on all the buildings, and thousands of well-wishers lined the streets, filling the circle to overflowing.

Initially, the elevation of the city affected us a great deal. Located at an altitude of over 1,850 meters (6,069 feet), Hamadan was a few hundred meters higher than Denver. Living there required much adjustment, and for weeks, always tired, we dragged ourselves around the neighborhood, crashing for naps every afternoon, hoping to find the energy to continue our busy schedules.

We were housed in the former Presbyterian Mission hospital, which the Iranian government had recently purchased. Our rooms were the former hospital wards, big and barn-like with almost no furniture except for simple metal cots. On the hospital grounds, I discovered a small cemetery with the graves of former missionaries and medical personnel. A lonely place, I thought, to spend eternity. Two of the missionaries, Jack and Phyllis Bird from San Francisco, still occupied their big house near the hospital, and Peace Corps Volunteers often gathered there, I learned, to celebrate the holidays, especially Thanksgiving.

We did our practice teaching in a government school off Bu Ali Sina Street. As we walked up and down the steep avenue, we passed the monument to Avicenna (Bu Ali Sina or Ibn Sina), one of Iran's most illustrious scholars, who died in the city in 1037 CE. On this same street stood the Hotel Bu Ali, a fine establishment, surrounded by a luxurious garden with a swimming pool tucked away out of sight. One could sit and while away the hours in this cool, shady space, perhaps ordering the famous Chicken Kiev, or simply a Shams beer and Iranian pistachios. In the evening, after a long day of teaching, language classes, lectures on various subjects, many of us would unwind in the hotel garden.

It is worth pointing out that centuries ago Iranians mastered the art of creating beautiful walled gardens, places of refuge from a harsh landscape. They provide one of the country's unexpected delights. The word "paradise" comes from an ancient Persian word, meaning "walled enclosure," and these gardens, large and small, offer a kind of paradise, found everywhere across the country. They always feature running water, either from fountains or in open channels, which seems so pleasant after a long journey through hot, dusty, dry landscapes. They provide pleasure and relaxation to all, whether it be the famous, elaborate gardens of the Bagh-e Fin in Kashan or the humble green space in a small town.

Alcohol was widely available then, although many Iranians did not imbibe. I was always impressed—and still am—at how much fun Iranians and other Muslims seemed to have without the addition of alcoholic beverages. Whereas, in the United States, we often rely on drinks to loosen things up and get the party rolling, Muslim acquaintances over the years have not exhibited this same learned behavior. In almost five and a half years in Iran, I never saw an inebriated Iranian in public.

Some establishments, especially those in large cities or at tourist locations, would sell alcohol openly, others under the counter. When I lived in Mashhad (1971-1973) after my Peace Corps service, I would go to an Armenian sandwich shop to buy beer or vodka, none of which was on display. After paying the cashier, I would walk down the block to be met by a clerk carrying my brown paper bag. Such transactions were an open secret.

An essential element in our training was the lectures on health and hygiene presented by Peace Corps Nurse Terry Maurella. She warned us off many foods, lettuce and strawberries were high on her list, anything that could not be washed thoroughly or soaked in solution. We should also avoid buying food from street vendors, she cautioned, even the cooked variety. She related many horror stories of PCVs, who had failed to heed her advice and suffered accordingly.

Volunteers regularly experienced upset stomachs; even those who took considerable care with their diets might suffer. Giardia was a frequent companion. When the malady bordered on dysentery, one or more Lomotil tablets became our dearest friends; they seemed to calm even the worst episodes of stomach cramps and diarrhea. Too much of the magic tablet, of course, could lead to the opposite problem. We tried to achieve the perfect—but elusive— balance. Every six months or so, we received gamma globulin injections to boost our immune systems and help to ward off infections such as hepatitis A. What were we to do, we wondered, when our Iranian hosts offered us a fresh green salad or some other forbidden fruit? "Just tell them you have an allergy," Terry remarked. She offered sensible advice, aimed to protect us, but often neglected. And we paid the inevitable price.

No sooner had nurse Terry delivered her medical admonitions, than a quite different Terry took the podium. Terrence O'Donnell leaned heavily on his cane, a constant companion since a childhood automobile accident left him disabled. He presented a contrasting introduction to Iran. Whereas the nurse saw dangers lurking everywhere, he urged us to embrace all that the country had to offer, including its street food. This Terry, a longtime American expatriate, had become something of a mystic during his years in Shiraz and its environs. He advised us to slow down, to enjoy the more relaxed pace of life. Live more in the moment, he advised. He saw only positive experiences wherever he turned. This Terry would become a firm friend in the years ahead.

But clearly the most important in-country staff member, at least in the short term, was Dr. Gertrude Nye Dorry, who directed the TEFL program for the Peace Corps. Another American expatriate, she had married an Iranian bureaucrat. She had a fearsome reputation among the volunteers, tough as nails and undeviating in her devotion to the aural-oral method of teaching English. She drilled the basic concepts into our heads during those intensive four weeks in Hamadan. She cautioned us never to use Persian in the classroom, which we would be tempted to do. That would be the easy route, but, she cautioned, it would be a disservice to our students. Unlike O'Donnell, Dr. Dorry castigated what she considered the lethargy and incompetence of many Iranian officials, especially many who worked for the Ministry of Education.

She and her staff of Volunteers taught us the fundamentals of making pocket charts and other visual aids for the classroom. These humble skills would come in handy at our sites, where everything had to be constructed from scratch. We learned various techniques for a variety of classroom language drills. They also observed and critiqued our classes, which could be a nerve-wracking experience.

We peppered these seasoned Volunteers with questions about their lives in Iran, scrambling to gather as much information as we could in the short time available. What wisdom could they impart to us? It soon became apparent that they had had a range of experiences, both good and bad, and we were left to pick and choose from what they offered.

I particularly enjoyed being able at last to practice my rudimentary Persian in real conversations. Iranians always seemed surprised—and pleased, I think—that a foreigner had made the effort to learn their language. In training we had been introduced to all the important grammatical constructions, and now it was our job to practice what we had been taught. I liken this to the biblical story about seeds cast on fertile soil versus those on barren ground. Some took root, others did not. In bigger cities, many Iranians spoke English better than volunteers spoke Persian and so language skills tended to wither.

One new word soon became etched in my mind. *Bastani* is the Persian word for ice cream, for which I had a great fondness. I remember well my first encounter with the local variety. One blisteringly hot day in Hamadan, three of us stopped at an ice cream shop, and we each ordered a cone; mine was chocolate. With much anticipation I took a big bite, my taste buds prepared for what they thought they were about to experience. Wrong! The flavor sensations were like nothing I had ever tasted, for the ice cream was made with rosewater, and suddenly that unusual, and not altogether pleasant, flavor filled my mouth. I did my best to finish the cone, but it would be some time before I tried another.

A more pleasant experience came when I visited the covered bazaar in Hamadan for the first time. These traditional marketplaces, not only in Iran but throughout the Middle East, were organized in similar fashion. All the shops devoted to a particular item, such as shoes, pots and pans, spices, and so forth, were located in the same area. Perfect competition, or so it seemed. I particularly remember the section full of shops selling gold jewelry and brass items, such as samovars, candlesticks, and an infinite variety of trays. Everything glistened under countless tiny lights. The brass objects had been shined to perfection. Keeping tarnish at bay was the job of young boys, who were attached to each enterprise. It all made a startling impression. Whenever I came back to Hamadan, I always found time to wander through the brass bazaar, and from time to time I even made purchases.

As the weeks passed, I became more confident in the classroom, and my language skills quickly improved. Like young birds in the nest, we were being prepared for solo flights. In one exercise, the staff sent us out in pairs to distant locations to see how we would cope. Dennis Ghyst and I drew the desert city of Kashan, where we encountered temperatures well above the century mark. Phil Schwarz was the Volunteer there, and he kindly showed us around. After two days, we returned exhausted but proud of our achievement.

Soon, everyone in our group was offered a position, some in large cities others in small towns of a few thousand inhabitants. The staff offered me the town of Shahindezh in Western Azerbaijan province. The population there consisted largely of Azeri Turks and Kurds. I had already spoken with enough old hands to know that it would be difficult to master Persian, living in a region where that was not the mother tongue of most of the population. I worried that after two years' service, I would come away with a smattering of several languages but mastery of none. I had reluctantly given up my hopes of serving in a French-speaking country, at least I should have every opportunity to learn the lingua franca of Iran. I had this idea fixed in my head, so I asked for an alternate site, one in a purely Persian-speaking region.

I soon found myself on an introductory visit to Tuyserkan, a town of approximately fourteen thousand inhabitants, which lay on the opposite side of Mount Alvand (elevation, 3,581 meters/11,750 ft.) from Hamadan. Tuyserkan was off the beaten path, on the direct road to nowhere. To get there I had to take a shared taxi, which took about ninety minutes in good weather to cover the ninety kilometers. First, we headed south on the road toward Malayer and then turned west at the small village of Jokar. From there a gravel road stretched out before us. In the dry season—as it was that August—dense clouds of dust followed us across the plain. If two vehicles should pass going in opposite directions, their drivers would be temporarily blinded. Pray that at that critical juncture no slower vehicle appeared in the road ahead. Sometimes there would be horrific crashes out in the middle of nowhere, and you would wonder how that could have happened for normally one could see miles in any direction. One of the Peace Corps field officers, Charlie Duncan, was severely injured in such a collision while he was passing a slow-moving vehicle in a cloud of dust.

From Jokar, the road crossed an empty plain, then, after a slight rise, it began a steep descent into a well-defined valley. The road wound down to the valley floor in a series of gentle loops. As you descended, you could look down the length of the valley, past the gardens marking the course of the Sarabi River and the green irrigated lands that stretched as far as Khan Goremaz (The King Cannot See), the solitary mountain that sat at the western end of the valley.[1] Dozens of villages large and small, with a cumulative population of perhaps two hundred thousand, dotted the plain. The town itself seemed hardly more than a village from that distance. At the very last curve in the road, Gazandar Bala, stood a teahouse where the rushing river passed under the roadway. This was a favorite spot for picnicking and other merriment. From here the road ran straight as an arrow for several kilometers to the outskirts of Tuyserkan.

I remember many outings with friends and their families on hot summer days at Gazandar, which was always cooler than the town. The young children, both boys and girls, would frolic in the cold mountain stream dressed only in their briefs, while the adults enjoyed kebabs and other refreshments on the bank. After long walks and sometimes afternoon naps under the trees, we would return late in the evening to town. What a refreshing break for everyone.

A small, newly constructed rotary with grass and flowers announced the formal entrance into the town. From there a broad, straight, asphalted street ran one half mile, abruptly returning to

---

[1] This Turkish name had been applied to the mountain because its summit was often shrouded in a ring of cloud.

gravel as one exited the far end of the town. Homes and, then further on, shops lined both sides of the street. A shorter road crossed
the main thoroughfare at a right angle at the central square, which
was the center of activity. Only the portion to the right, leading up-
hill toward the gardens had been asphalted. From this intersection,
the entrance to the small, covered bazaar could be seen and towering
over that the minarets of the Jomeh (Friday) mosque.

Along each side of the asphalted roads ran a concrete or earth-
en channel (*joob*) approximately two feet deep and a foot wide.
These were designed to carry away rainwater and snowmelt and
were found everywhere in Iran. Local authorities regularly flushed
them to remove any accumulation of trash. It was not uncommon
for newcomers, such as me, to stumble into one of these, causing
considerable embarrassment.

At the entrance to the town, in a small but tranquil walled garden to the left of the roadway stood the three-story Hotel Alvand. It
was an excellent establishment, a real gem, better than many in
much larger towns.   It boasted clean, bright, and airy rooms, and
excellent food. During the day, one could enjoy the garden with
only the peaceful sounds of a small fountain breaking the silence;
with nightfall came diners' voices, radio music, and occasionally
Hajji's loud command to the kitchen staff from his perch near the
open gate.

Hajji, the only name I ever knew him by, was the proud proprietor. He was a character. He had not yet made the pilgrimage to
Mecca, but rather had a birth date that allowed him to use that hon-
orific. Short and stout with an unshaven look, his eyes appeared
lively and penetrating. He was the only Iranian I ever knew with
more than one wife; he had two, one, an older woman, the other
much younger. Between them they had seven children. The wives
each lived in their own quarters. Wives and children seemed to
work endlessly to maintain the hotel. They cleaned and cooked, and
the children ran constant errands in town for their father. Heaven
help the young ones if they incurred their father's wrath. He would
berate them loudly or even cuff them about the ears. Amid the bustle, Hajji would stop to chat with guests, sometimes sitting with
them as a sign of his regard. Perhaps, he would order something
special for them from the kitchen. One night, much later, he served
my friends and me a platter of *dombalan*, sheep's testicles, sliced
and fried to perfection. We appreciated the gesture.   He was a
shrewd businessman.

I stayed at the hotel during my first, short visit to Tuyserkan. It was so pleasant inside the walls that I had to steel myself to go outside, but I knew that I must. Iranians have a wonderful tradition called the *gardesh*, which consists of a long, stroll through parks or along public thoroughfares in good weather with friends or family. In Tuyserkan, the one sealed road became the locus of the *gardesh* each afternoon as the sun began to decline, temperatures cooled, and residents awoke from their naps. The divided street filled with people, two streams moving in opposite directions ever so slowly. It would take a group at least a half hour, perhaps longer to cover the distance of the asphalted roadway. Then they would turn and move back in the direction from which they had come. They would nod and acknowledge passersby moving in the opposite direction. Sometimes a member of one group would stop to talk, and the other group members would move on. Perhaps, he would catch up with them or he might join with a different group and move in the opposite direction. As an American, I found it especially difficult to slow my pace of walking. We tend to walk with such urgency even when at leisure. It took a long time to master the art of walking slowly.

During the *gardesh*, male friends might hold hands as they strolled down the avenue. This signified nothing more than strong friendship. Although I came to master the glacially slow walk, I never became comfortable holding an Iranian friend's hand.

My entrée into Tuyserkan society came on a Friday afternoon during the *gardesh*. I determined to walk, alone, to the end of the boulevard and back. This proved to be the most nerve-wracking experience of my life. As I headed down one side of the avenue alone, forcing myself not to move too quickly, all eyes turned in my direction. People would stop and stare (staring was not considered impolite). As I passed carpenters, cobblers, and tin smiths, I could hear their tools fall silent. Clearly, the tradesmen were gazing at this new blonde American spectacle in their midst. I could hear the sounds of hammering and sawing cease and then resume. Sweat poured down my sides, not from the August heat but from nervousness. I struggled to keep my outward composure, as I called out, *Salaam* (hello), to those I passed. Reaching the end of the road, I turned slowly, smiling all the while as I moved back toward the hotel. It took a conscious effort not to quicken my pace on the return trip. Finally, I arrived at the hotel gate, my sanctuary. I had survived my first ordeal.

As the Peace Corps had not yet officially assigned me to Tuyserkan, I did not make any formal contacts or introductions during that brief stay. I did, however, explore the town a little further the next day. I visited the tomb of Habakkuk, the biblical prophet, which lay in the middle of wheat fields just outside town. Stylistically, the solitary, brick tomb resembled the architecture of the Seljuq period of the 11th-12th centuries. At the center of town, shops in the small, unpretentious covered bazaar sold only basic necessities. Overall, I liked what I saw and returned to Hamadan determined to accept the posting. This was easily arranged.

Within ten days, the training program ended with the taking of oaths. We said our farewells to fellow PCVs and staff, and with a sense of excitement and anxiousness headed off to assigned sites in various parts of Iran. I had, perhaps, the shortest distance to travel.

Rhythms of A New Life

The Office of Education in Tuyserkan knew of my assignment and had arranged to rent a house for me. It was a newer construction, much bigger than I needed; a teacher owned it, and he had been transferred to Tehran, so I became his tenant. The house was located at some distance from the main thoroughfare down a winding maze of *kuchehs* or alleyways. Most of the people in the town lived along *kuchehs*, which were dirt lanes. In the dry season they were fine, but after rain or snow, they would become muddy and difficult to navigate. The doctors and more important bureaucrats lived along one or the other of the two paved streets.

My new house was a single-story structure with a brick façade, and a flat, adobe roof like most of the other buildings in the town. The front gate opened directly onto the *kucheh*, and inside the courtyard there was a narrow passageway around three sides of the house. To the left of the front gate stood the *mostarat* (WC), consisting of a small room with a hole in the cement floor and a water spigot. At the back of the house was a large, open space. An eight-foot adobe wall surrounded the entire compound. No passer-by could peer into my yard. The large courtyard at the back was quite empty as the owner had not yet planted a garden. It contained only one or two scraggly fruit trees and a small shallow pool (*hoz*), several feet in diameter, sometimes used for washing clothes.

Inside, a long hallway, open at both ends, ran down the middle of the house. With no doors to keep them out, I would occasionally find a scorpion slinking along the wall. Those encounters gave us both a surprise. To the right of the hallway was a large storage room, a kitchen, and a shower room. To the left stood a small guest room and next to it a large room with windows facing onto the courtyard. This became my bedroom and study.

Volunteers had served in Tuyserkan since 1964. First had come Don Burkhart, who left a reputation as an avid hiker. Then came Larry Atkins followed by Steve Hill, Barbara Johnson, and Richard Sullivan in 1966. I inherited a number of items they had left in storage, including a bed and dresser, a double burner gas ring, a small metal oven which fitted over the burners for baking, and a *korsi*.[2]

It quickly became clear that I would stand in the shadow of my predecessors until I could make my own place in the town. People constantly asked me questions about those who had come before, praising them to the skies. This grated on me somewhat, but I suppose it was to be expected. Those earlier volunteers were like my extended family. They were known quantities; I was not.

I also inherited Turon, who had worked for Sullivan. She came pounding on my metal gate as soon as she heard a new Volunteer had arrived. It took me a while to understand who she was, for my Persian was still limited, and she had a speech impediment, which added to my difficulty. I guess there was never any doubt, at least in her mind, that she would become my cook and housekeeper. She came from one of the distant villages, but she was no stranger to Tuyserkan. My Iranian friends later told me something of her background. She had apparently been hired as a girl to work for the family of the local landed magnate, where she also was expected to provide sexual experiences for the young sons of the household. After a number of years, the family found her an older husband in the village, and she left their employ. She and Fazollah started their own family raising two daughters. The older daughter, whom I never met, married and stayed in the village, the younger daughter, Fathi, lived with her parents on the outskirts of town. Turon always spoke of the landholder's family with much respect.

She dressed in layers of clothing; she covered her head with a white scarf. Short in stature, she almost disappeared into her assorted garments. She had jet black hair, but showing henna at the roots, and a ruddy complexion. I had no idea how old she was, and she might not have known that herself.

---

[2] See, page 38, for an explanation of this term.

Initially, I had had no intention of hiring a housekeeper, but it soon became apparent just how practical this arrangement could be. There was no prepared food in the town, no restaurant except the hotel. Everything had to be made from scratch each day, for refrigerators were just beginning to appear in homes. Besides, Iranians did not savor leftovers; usually, any surplus went to servants or to the poor.

Thus, each morning, wives and mothers or their servants would head to the central square where they would bargain for vegetables, meat, yoghurt and other staples. Beef or lamb carcasses would hang on hooks in butcher shops and customers would haggle to obtain the best quality at the lowest price. Butchers would favor some customers over others. Friends told me that their elderly father would always pay less for whatever he bought than any of his grown sons. For chicken, one could choose from an array of birds running around in the dust in front of you. Pick one up in your hand, thump the breast up and down and make your decision. The bird could be slaughtered on the spot or later at home. Whatever the choice, preparation included pouring boiling water over the carcass to remove the feathers and then plucking by hand. All of this took time. Locals lauded the superior quality of free-range chickens versus what they called "Machine" chickens, those raised somewhere en masse in enclosures. In the end, my chicken dishes were usually stringy and tough.

As I would be teaching most days, there would be little time for food preparation. Hiring Turon meant a hot meal when I came home for the long midday break, and I could also invite friends to lunch or dinner. She would prepare meat and vegetable stews (*khoresh*), platters of long-grained rice—Iranian rice was the finest anywhere—mixed with dried fruit, meat and vegetables (*pilaf*), and occasionally thick soups (*osh*) and, more rarely, kebabs. Bread came from the local bakery. Although one could find a variety of unleavened breads in Iran, in Tuyserkan *nun-e sangak* (literally, "bread of little stones") predominated. It got its name from the fact that the whole wheat dough was spread out in the oven over a layer of hot stones. Each unleavened "loaf" was about four feet long and ten inches wide. You had to take care when eating that no stones lay hidden in the bread. This variety was delicious when first baked but needed to be eaten soon after purchase, otherwise it quickly became tough or dry.

If a piece of bread somehow fell unnoticed to the ground, a passerby would pick it up and place it on a nearby wall, making it available for anyone in need. It would never be thrown away; that was considered sinful.

Turon would also do my laundry, boiling water in tubs over an open fire in the courtyard, or when I had hot water, washing the clothes on the tiled floor of the bathroom. She did light housekeeping, using a broom of local plant material to sweep the inexpensive *ziloos* (pileless textiles) on the bedroom and living room floors. Although everyone removed their shoes upon entering a home, dust collected everywhere.

One of her last acts each day during the hot summer months was to hose down the dusty courtyard and the split-bamboo *hasirs* (blinds), which covered all the windows. The moisture would quickly evaporate, causing a noticeable cooling on the inside of the house. I can still remember the lovely aroma which arose from the wetted surfaces at day's end.

I soon learned that employing a housekeeper implied certain obligations on my part. In addition to paying her monthly salary of sixty *tomans* (7.5 t. = $1US), at the Iranian new year, March 20, the vernal equinox, I provided money for a new set of clothes for Turon and her daughter for the coming year and also a cash bonus to meet various expenses associated with new year celebrations. Later, when Fazollah died, I would send money for tea and sugar to be served to mourners, who came to pay their respects at her home. This was all a novel arrangement for me, one that I could not have imagined and for which I had absolutely no preparation.

I learned as I went along, and over time, we became quite fond of each other. She worked hard, and she had to put up with my occasional moodiness. My friends would sometimes tease her good-naturedly. Whenever she became upset or surprised, she would whack the back of one hand with the palm of the other, saying in a raised voice, "*Ak-e Heh,*" indicating, I imagined, some degree of astonishment. Before her husband died, if she neglected to do something I had asked her to do, she would tell me that she forgot because she was so worried about his poor health; after he died when she neglected to do something, she would tell me that she could not keep her mind on her work because she was so upset over his death.

After three years together, I offered to take her and Fathi with me to my new job in Mashhad on the other side of Iran. Turon was horrified at the thought and told me that her son-in-law would divorce her daughter if Turon were to leave the area. I never understood that concern, but I respected her decision. Her world was narrowly circumscribed. I think she found it impossible to conceive of the broad world that lay beyond the Tuyserkan valley. Once when I was preparing to return to the States for a home visit after my first two years, I told Turon that I was going home to America. She pointed to the mountains to the south, asking, "Is *Amrika* on the other side of those?"

My next-door neighbor, Mr. Sadr, was a religious scholar, a kind man. He dressed in a traditional *'aba* (cloak) and taught religion classes at Shahpur High School. The older boys there often made fun of him, but he ignored them. Whenever he spoke to me, he took great care to enunciate each Persian syllable as if that would guarantee my understanding. He had two teen-aged sons, and I became quite friendly with the older one, Seyed.

I remember when he lived next door, Seyed used to visit often, and sometimes he would bring game which he had shot, such as rabbits, for Turon to prepare. His father adhered strictly to the detailed Islamic dietary laws. In his house they did not prepare rabbit nor many kinds of game birds that were forbidden. Thus, Seyed was able to come secretly and eat his kill in my house. There was also briefly another volunteer in Tuyserkan that first year, Mark Munkittrick, who shared the house and of whom Seyed was very fond. Mark came to do community development work, but after a few months he decided to leave for Tehran to be reassigned.

After graduation, Seyed went into the Sepah-e danesh, the Literacy Corps, and he served in a village outside Miandoab in the north. The shah set up this program as part of the White Revolution in 1963; high school graduates could teach in village schools in lieu of military service. It seemed to be working well for Seyed. We corresponded several times after he left, and I saw him again when he came home on leave.

During these early days in Tuyserkan, I suffered a lot of stomach cramps and diarrhea, which complaints were universal among new Volunteers. One never wanted to be far from a WC. Fortunately, Iranians had many answers for upset stomachs. They recommended *kateh*, plain white rice, and yoghurt. And, of course, tea. I became quite a tea drinker. Normally, guests would drink a glass or two out of politeness; I took to drinking endless glasses. I could empty a samovar of its water. Among my friends, this became a subject of occasional merriment, at my expense.

Outside the home, there was a whole class of employees devoted to the preparation and serving of tea. Teahouses were everywhere; some of them were quite elaborate. Laborers gathered there, and traditional storytellers could often be found on the premises, relaying tales of ancient heroes and their exploits. Generally, Iranians did not drink coffee. It was difficult to find a good cup outside the capital. Tea was their specialty. Every office building either had its own tearoom from whence trays of tea would be delivered to various offices throughout the day or officials would order tea from a nearby teahouse. No place of business was more than a few meters from one of these. For whatever reason, the drinking of tea spread far wider than coffee, and some version of the word "chai" is understood all the way from China to southeastern Europe.

Iranians also had sensible prescriptions for various other maladies. They divided foods into hot and cold categories. Depending on the ailment, they would prescribe one food group or another. This represented longstanding practices, but I never understood what I should or should not eat when I had a cold, for example. I horrified my friends when I ate *torshi*—pickled vegetables—all the time, even when I had a cold. This violated all the rules. I just loved pickled cauliflowers, garlics, tomatoes, and so forth.

The school year formally began on September 23, although I quickly learned that serious work only started after the shah's birthday on October 26. Thus, I had several weeks to get everything in order. During that time, I introduced myself to various members of the Ehsani family, who had become particularly good friends with the previous volunteers. This extended family would be at the center of almost all my social relationships during the three years I lived in Tuyserkan. Their friends became my friends.

The elderly parents, Abibi and Doshanbe, were two of the most likable and hospitable individuals I have ever known. Doshanbe had retired from his clerking in the local taxation office and received a small government pension. Each morning he rose early to shop in the bazaar for whatever his wife required for the day's meals. I would often encounter the slightly built old man with the grizzled beard as I made my way to school. Abibi, like all the women in the town, wore her *chador* (veil) whenever outside her home and inside she often had it wrapped around her stooped shoulders. Although she had little formal education and came from a religiously conservative family, she always showed great interest in what was happening in places beyond Tuyserkan. She asked me many questions about my family and life in America. I think she always felt sorry for me because I was so far from home. Their six grown children, four boys and two girls, showed them great love and respect as did others in the community.

They lived humbly. When I first met them, they resided in an old, two-story wood and adobe house on one of the *kuchehs* near the main square. A wooden balcony connected the rooms lined up in a row on the second floor. Each room had French doors. The single large living room rarely received direct sunlight. The kitchen was in a separate location along the balcony. The traditional toilet or WC was located on the ground floor. For bathing, like many of those in town, they would go to the nearest public bathhouse or *hammam*.

Weekly bathing was a lengthy process. Women would sometimes bring their laundry with them. They would meet friends, talk endlessly, gossip and drink tea. There were steam rooms, where customers could obtain a massage, and a large, shallow pool for cooling off. Men and women went separately through this process; certain days were set aside for women and children. In-home showers were beginning to appear in newer houses in the town and attendance at the traditional Persian baths was declining. The more modern set often considered going to the traditional baths old fashioned and even somewhat primitive.

The elder Ehsanis had lived at this address for many years and had raised all their children in this same space. All of the children, but one, had earned higher education degrees; five of them were teachers or school administrators. This was a remarkable testament of the parents' commitment to education and to raising the status of the family.

Their eldest son, Mashollah and his wife Mahvash and their two sons, Saeed and Masoud, (their daughter, Mahtab, would be born during my time in Tuyserkan.) lived in a new home on the main avenue. "Ehsani," as we all called him, was an amazing man. He had won a US Fulbright teacher education grant and had spent a number of months in Salt Lake City, Utah, which he had thoroughly enjoyed. He told me that when he had arrived in Utah in midwinter, he was amazed to see the grocery stores with every kind of fruit and vegetable on display. He thought he had died and gone to heaven, he said, because according to Muslim tradition only in heaven would such produce be available all year round. In those years, produce in Iran was still limited by the season. During my third year in Iran, he would receive a fellowship from the British Council and spend the academic year, 1970-1971, in London.

By the time I arrived in Tuyserkan, he had been appointed principal of one of the two boys' high schools in town, after a number of years in the classroom. He was an excellent administrator and widely respected. He had a calm and thoughtful manner, and people often sought him out for advice.

As the eldest brother, he had the final word with any of his siblings, but even within the family, where tradition guaranteed his authority, he achieved his ends not by imposing his own ideas on his brothers and sisters but by patiently trying to convince them to do what he wanted. I frequently witnessed him using these same skills on unruly students. Rather than dictating to them, which he could easily have done, he tried to show them why their behavior was unacceptable and to convince them that they should be embarrassed by what they had done.

Ehsani also had a wonderful sense of humor. I remember how he would occasionally tease his mother-in-law, Ghamar-khanum, who came from a much more religiously conservative background than his own. He did not spare his friends either, including me.

I spent many happy times in his home. Mahvash was very welcoming, joining in all our conversations, while the children crawled in and out of their parents' laps. We sat cross-legged on cushions on the heavily carpeted floor with our backs against the wall for support. Although most newer homes sported a separate Western-style dining room with suitable tables and chairs, these saw little use except on very formal occasions. Tuyserkanis still preferred to sit as they had always done. They also ate their meals from cloths (*sofreh*) laid over the carpets and at the end of the evening they rolled out bedding to sleep on the carpeted floor as well.

Nasrollah, a few years younger than Ehsani, served as principal of an elementary school. He was something of a black sheep in the family, having divorced his first wife. Divorce was not looked on kindly especially as Nasrollah had a young daughter, Minoo, who was now solely his responsibility. Partly for that reason, he married again shortly after my arrival in town. Even then, he spent many of his evenings away from home, playing cards and partying with friends. His parents were not pleased, and they told him so.

I spent more time with Mansur, the third brother, than with the others combined. He was only a few years older than me, and he, too, was single. He had been very friendly with the other volunteers, especially Rick Sullivan.   Mansur taught in Emir Kabir High School, where his brother was principal.   He was finishing his college degree at Tehran University during my first two years there, so there were long periods when he would be away.   He talked from time to time about going to the United States to further his studies, but nothing ever came of this idea.   He was a good friend and helped me adjust to life in Tuyserkan in many ways.   I spent many evenings with him and his friends, playing cards—more often watching them playing cards—talking, drinking vodka made in Malayer, having dinner at Gazandar Bala or perhaps attending the one cinema in town.

Iranian cinema was just beginning to develop a reputation for fine films. "Gav" (The Cow, 1969) was one I particularly remember, the quality being so much better than the usual fare at the theater.   Indian films seemed to attract large audiences.   Each showing began with the playing of the national anthem, the *Surud-e Shahanshahi Iran* (The Imperial Salute of Iran). Everyone was expected to stand silently until the end.   I joined with the others but always felt a little awkward in doing so.   Years later I read that in the months leading up to the revolution many moviegoers remained in their seats, a sure sign of disrespect for the monarch.

Tuyserkan had no television service, so this small cinema provided the only modern entertainment other than the radio.   Not everyone considered going to the cinema an acceptable pastime; it drew the local bureaucrats, many teachers and government representatives, but many conservative folks disapproved and stayed away.

In the lobby there was a small sandwich kiosk. I remember well one night buying and eating a *kalbas* (sausage) sandwich on our way out after the show.   Fortunately, several friends had stopped by my house before heading home.   As we sat and talked, suddenly an intense bubble of indigestion began to swell in my chest, and soon I could hardly breathe, the pain was intense.   Fortunately, they knew exactly what to do.   One of them raced to the pharmacy and got a tablet to release the gas.   I no sooner took the tablet than a huge belch came forth, and the emergency was over.   I do not know what might have happened if I had been alone.   I was sincerely grateful.   The sandwich meat must have spoiled.   They were reluctant to leave me, even though I told them that the threat had passed, and they could go home.   Two of them stayed the night just to be sure the crisis was over.

I had little access to information from outside Tuyserkan. I could not receive English language broadcasts on my inexpensive radio, nor were there any English language newspapers available. Even letters from the States were few and far between. My family members were not particularly committed letter writers. Any long-distance telephone calls within Iran had to be scheduled at the post office. I was told the connections were usually poor; I never made or received any calls. I did have a phone at home for local calls. This was powered by cranking a handle and then supplying a number to the operator. My only source of international news was my weekly copy of *Time* magazine, which regularly—if belatedly—found its way to the local post office. I papered my bedroom wall with three years of magazine covers.

I sometimes learned first of important events from friends, who relayed information from the radio and newspapers. When Apollo 14 landed on the moon, February 6, 1971, to be exact, Iranians were much more excited by this space venture than I was. Strangers congratulated me in the street. Only then did I learn the details of what had taken place.

During my time in Tuyserkan, we rarely discussed politics, but sometimes it was inevitable. Occasionally, someone would sound off about the United States and all the evil things it was doing in and to Iran. Mansur would often come to my defense, although he on occasion could voice his own concerns about all the military hardware, especially sophisticated and expensive aircraft, that the shah was buying from Washington. I did not feel responsible for my government's policies and yet, I was seen as the American representative, whether I liked it or not.

Then there were conversations about the virtues of communism compared to the American way of life. I was at a disadvantage here because we were always speaking Persian, and my fluency was limited to everyday, commonplace subjects. It was much harder to use higher level, abstract vocabulary. I was never sure if my interlocutors were serious about their professed admiration for communism or if they even understood it in any detail. Exasperated, I would observe that if that system were so wonderful why did communist governments need barbed-wire fences and guard posts to keep people from leaving.

Iran was the land of conspiracy theory. If anything went wrong, you would likely learn that the British or the CIA were behind the affair. In spite of the fact that Britain's power had declined considerably since the end of WWII, Iranians would attribute amazing influence to London's nefarious MI6, even going so far as to assume that the British could still get the Americans to do their bidding in the Middle East.

My friend, Nezeri, was a prime believer in conspiracies. He would question me about such issues as the relationship between Jack Ruby and Harvey Oswald, firmly convinced that JFK had been the victim of a plot.

Occasionally, Mansur and I would have disagreements over issues that later seemed rather trivial. I struggled to understand the expectations of Iranian friendship, and at times I wanted Mansur to behave like an American friend. There were bound to be misunderstandings. Sometimes I might feel sorry for myself and take out my frustrations on him. Sometimes we just had different approaches, which could not easily be reconciled. I recall once, for example, that we had traveled to Ghasr-e Shirin, a town on the Iraqi border to spend a long weekend with Mansur's sister and her family. We had a great stay, but when it was time to leave, I was the only one who insisted on going back for classes the next day. My view prevailed, but Mansur was not happy. We hardly spoke the entire trip back and for some time thereafter.

Later, Mansur bought an older home not far from Ehsani's on the main street, and his parents came to live with him there. It must have been hard for them to leave old friends and move to the new neighborhood, even though it was no more than a half mile away. Mansur had been considering marriage for some time; owning his own home would be an attractive feature of any proposal he might make.

Teimour, the youngest brother, was away fulfilling his military service in the Sepah-e danesh for much of my time there. He, I knew least of all. Yet, it was he, who took advantage of a widely practiced custom that troubled me at first. If someone admires something you own, you are bound to offer it to them by saying *pish kesh*, "it's yours." I wore an agate ring purchased in Iran, which Teimour admired one day. Without reflection, I offered it to him, and he took it. I was upset although I tried not to show it. I felt badly both for being so possessive over the ring, but also because I really liked it and wanted it back. He kept it for a few days before returning it. I think he was toying with me. Sometimes the exchange was permanent.

Older sister, Aroos, had married a religiously conservative man, Ali Murad Momtaz, from Malayer, and they and their children lived in that city. They came to Tuyserkan infrequently, although their two sons, Esmaeil and Ebrahim, often stayed with their grandparents, especially in the summer. From an early age, they showed a great interest in the foreigners.

Younger sister, Ashraf, had married Ghassem Bashiri, Ehsani's best friend, thus cementing that relationship. They lived in Ghasr-e Shirin with their two children, Mina and Homayoun. Ashraf taught in an elementary school, and Ghassem worked as an inspector for the Ministry of Education. Although I did not see them often, Ghassem became and has remained one of my best friends. Tall, handsome, and self-confident, he had an imposing presence, and people listened carefully to his views. He and Ehsani had done their teacher training together in Kermanshah in the early 1950s, when Mohammad Musaddiq was prime minister. Ghassem told me that he had supported that government, sometimes protesting or handing out fliers, but he felt that the situation had become too chaotic by August 1953. That was when the CIA had helped to overthrow the prime minister.

Tuyserkan was a rather conservative community. Only married men, for example, could teach in the girls' high school. Every woman in town wore the chador outside her home. There was only one exception to this and that was the district governor's wife, who went about her affairs without *hijab*. She also was the only woman who drove a car in the town. No one dared to openly disapprove, but many of the locals did not like the way she flouted local values.

Any noncompliance with local mores was done in the privacy of one's home or in the gardens above the town, where people tended to let their hair down a bit. In the larger cities and especially in Tehran there were many women without hijab, wearing the latest Western styles. It was easier for women to be anonymous there, and thus their behavior was less likely to reflect badly on their families, and that was all important.

When someone sought a marriage partner or a business partner, the reputation of their families was of critical importance. What kind of family did they come from? The individual's character played a role, but it seemed not nearly as important as in the United States. This was a regional phenomenon. When I was about to propose to my future wife, an Australian, a French acquaintance in Hamadan, the representative of the Oriental Carpet Company, who came from an old Beirut family, asked me what I knew about her family and warned me to take care.

In late September classes finally began. I had been assigned to teach in both boys' high schools, Shahpur and Emir Kebir. Each principal had a *nazem*, or assistant, who was responsible for enforcing the rules and disciplining students who broke them. Sometimes the *nazem* administered physical punishment. The administration at Shahpur was not effective, and the students could often be unruly. Emir Kebir had Ehsani as principal and his good friend, Mansur Dabaghi, as *nazem*. They worked well together, and the students respected them both. This made my life much easier.

I had a total of seven classes of seventh and eighth grade students. The first year (7th grade) students had no previous experience with English, and the curriculum required they take four hours each week. The classes were so big, sometimes as many as sixty or seventy students, that it was difficult to make much progress. I tried to use numbers to advantage by dividing the students into groups for recitation and especially for singing. Of course, this was like no activity they had ever encountered in school before. We would sing round robins of "Row, Row, Row Your Boat" and "Mary Had a Little Lamb." They always seemed to enjoy those sessions. I know some of my fellow instructors considered such goings-on rather silly and unbecoming a "real" teacher.

Teachers were often distant, austere figures; their charges should respect them. Students sprang to their feet and stood silent when the instructor entered the room, and then he or she would motion them to sit. Rote learning was the norm. Iranian students could memorize volumes of material and recite it almost verbatim. But what I expected them to do, enter into discussion in English with each other or respond to my questions, tested them in new ways. My students always showed more aptitude for taking English dictation than for making conversation.

Dr. Dorry had instilled in us the basics of the aural-oral method of instruction, and we were warned against resorting to Persian in the classroom. For several months I tried valiantly to stick with the regimen, but eventually—and with considerable guilt—I decided to use Persian at certain key points, especially when introducing new grammar. It seemed to help some of the students, who had been having great difficulty keeping up. Using Persian was no panacea, for the large numbers of students and the few hours of English class per week, almost dictated snail-like progress for most of the students. I think they did enjoy coming up to the front of the class for a brief conversation or working with the pocket chart to turn statements into questions.

Classrooms had few furnishings. There was a simple slate blackboard. The only decoration on the walls was a picture of the shah above the blackboard at the front. Students sat on long benches behind long rows of desks. Thus, the pictures I brought to class would have added some interest.

Of course, as I relaxed the usual rules of an Iranian classroom, maintaining discipline became more of a problem. At Emir Kebir I had support but that was lacking at the other high school where I was pretty much on my own. And some days I would get so stressed that I would come home and cry in frustration. Fortunately, this did not happen often. Wintertime was the worst for it was cold and the only heating in the crowded classrooms was provided by a *bokhari*. This was an upright metal drum fitted with a burner and a small tank of kerosene that would drip to feed the burner once the stove had been lit. There was no protection from the hot metal drum, so the students had to keep their distance. Sometimes I would come into a classroom at Shahpur and find that one or more students had opened the spigot wide, resulting in a raging fire and a red-hot stove. It would be vibrating madly. I would have to turn the spigot to normal position and sometimes evacuate the students while I did so. This, of course, whittled away class time. At other times, students would toss some material onto the top of the stove, often chewing gum or a rubber band, and it would melt, releasing unpleasant smells. Again, we would temporarily evacuate the classroom for the fresh air outside. Fortunately, this never happened at Emir Kebir.

Although many of the students came from the town, a considerable number came from the villages. Just to attend classes regularly required much effort on their part. A village boy from Sirkan or Artiman, two of the nearest villages, might have to walk a half hour or more each way to and from the high school. And they still had all their chores to do. That would mean rising at sunrise to take the livestock out to pasture and bringing them back in the evening. Then they had their homework to complete. No wonder some of them had difficulty keeping up with the work. I can imagine their conversations with their parents when they talked about their unusual language classes and the bizarre *Amrika'i* who taught them.

Somewhat surprisingly some of my best students came from the villages. Many of the town boys tended to be less focused on their studies. The villagers seemed more serious generally and, on the whole, more respectful.

Mansur Dabaghi, the *nazem* at Emir Kebir, became a good friend. He was married to a religiously conservative woman, and they had three daughters, when I knew him. Later, they had a fourth child, a son. Mansur's wife frowned on the activities of our group of friends and our frequent evening entertainments. She tried to keep her husband close to home. They owned a garden above the town, and Mansur enjoyed above all else working on his land, where he had many fruit and nut trees. Tuyserkan was famous for its almonds, walnuts and apricots. Mansur also raised vegetables, including garlic, which we often ate fresh from the field. At that early stage, it had none of the strong taste that it would later acquire.

Many a night we gathered at his garden, where he had a small one-room adobe building. We would spend our time outside under the stars and sometimes sleep there as well under homemade quilts for it could be quite cool at such high elevation even in summer.

Families, who had plots in the gardens, would live there during the warmer months, only coming down into town occasionally, although the distance was not great. At night you could often hear solitary singers from a neighboring vineyard or orchard, their melodious voices trailing over the hills. When they grew silent, the dogs, coyotes and occasionally a wolf could be heard further up the mountainside.

Mansur suffered from ulcers; he was not supposed to smoke or drink, but he did both. Perhaps, being the chief disciplinarian was not the best job for someone with his complaints. The students held him in high respect, and only occasionally did one of them step out of line. I remember one day looking out my classroom window to see a senior student streaking across the courtyard and disappearing out the school gate. Hot on his heels came Mansur, which presented an unusual sight, for Iranian adult men rarely sprinted for any reason; it showed a lack of decorum. Apparently, the offending student, who had quite a record of misbehaving, had uttered some flippant comment in response to the *nazem*'s chastisement. That was enough to set off the chase. The offending student was expelled, but he was allowed to enroll at the other high school.

During the hot summer months, residents who remained in towns such as Tuyserkan and especially those in crowded urban areas, would often sleep on their rooftops. Whether on the roof or in the courtyard, they set up large wooden platforms, where bedding would be spread and over all, mosquito netting, which would rest on the four posts of the platform. This provided a pleasant alternative to sleeping inside. It meant rising early in the morning with the sun, but that would not be a problem for devout Muslims, who would pray at that time anyway.

I worked hard during my three years in town. I spent long evenings and weekends grading student work and devising various activities for future classes. I made all of my own teaching aids. I was pretty much on my own as far as instruction was concerned. Once or twice a year a Peace Corps field officer would visit, and sometimes he would bring a visitor from the States, who might be carrying out research on the impact of Peace Corps teaching or some similar project.

On one of these visits, the field officer and I were riding in his jeep toward the village of Oshtoron. As we came over a hilltop, there in front of us stood a herd of magnificent wild mountain sheep. These were rarely seen, and my mouth dropped open. Before I could say anything, however, he leaned on the horn, and they were gone in an instant. Why he did this I never understood. Perhaps, because he traveled so much, this was not an unusual sight for him. But I would never see such a herd again. I had no words to express my feelings at that moment.[3]

The only Iranian who visited my class in three years was the Director of Education for Hamadan province. He came once with his entourage, and the students went through some of their brief conversations with their beaming instructor looking on. The official photographer later sent me some photos of the occasion.

I did come to enjoy teaching in spite of the large classes and intermittent discipline problems. I enjoyed the challenge of organizing material to devise the best method for instruction. And the occasional glimmer in the eyes of an excited student provided enough encouragement to continue. All the while I was learning how to be a more effective teacher. I discovered that this was an endless journey. As a result of my experience in Tuyserkan, I decided to pursue a career in teaching.

All the teachers in the local schools were Muslim with two exceptions, me and an Assyrian Christian from Azerbaijan. How he

---

[3] The government has set up a reserve near Tuyserkan to protect this breed.

ended up in Tuyserkan, I never knew. Mr. Alghaws taught English, and the students gave him a really hard time. I must admit that he gave as good as he got, and it was not a healthy learning situation. In private conversations with me, he would constantly criticize the students, Muslims, and his fellow teachers in that order. Not surprisingly, he had a very sour outlook on life. I did not spend a lot of time with him. Occasionally, he would invite me to his home for lunch. He was married and had several young children. I noticed a marked difference in the food his wife prepared; her creations were much spicier than the usual Persian dishes. Every spring he fled Tuyserkan with his family for the ancestral village of Goegtapeh, where he spent the long summer months farming land he owned. I visited him there once, and he was like a changed man, so much more relaxed. He took me on a walk around the village, where only a minority of the population was then Christian. We visited an old friend of his, tending his vodka still. All his children had emigrated to the United States, a common phenomenon for Christian minorities throughout the Middle East. Eventually, Alghaws received his long-hoped for transfer to Tehran.

I was told that a Jewish family, parents and daughter, had lived in Tuyserkan a few years earlier. The father had a shop in the bazaar. One day, two peasants from a distant village appeared. He had done business with them before, so when the weather turned nasty, he invited them to stay the night in his home. Rumors abounded that he kept considerable wealth hidden in his house. During the night, the two peasants smothered their hosts and then searched for the supposed treasure. Finding none, they fled. Later, the police caught them. A friend of mine remembers seeing them being marched in shackles through the town.

In addition to my regular classes, I also started an evening class for young women. I am not sure how this all began, but it seemed to be an important outing for the several young women who attended regularly. They were all friends and teachers, and they laughed and tittered their way through each session. Any mispronunciation of Persian words on my part sent them into gales of laughter.

I also had English conversation times with two young doctors, who worked for the Ministry of Health. They followed each other in their appointments in Tuyserkan. Dr. Saboortinat and Dr. Yazdon-Bakhsh must have been fulfilling a government requirement by serving in such an isolated place. I assumed they had received government funding to complete their medical training. In any case they spent most of their time out in the villages; they did not have practices in the town. They would vaccinate villagers and treat their various medical complaints. From time to time there would be outbreaks of cholera or smallpox in one of the rural areas, and they would have to stay out in the villages as long as the crisis lasted. In winter 1971, several people had died of smallpox in nearby villages such as Gigion-kuh and everyone in town—including us Peace Corps Volunteers—had been inoculated. Although the doctors would rather have been elsewhere, it seemed to me that they were both very dedicated physicians. There was a permanent local staff, which assisted them in their labors. Given the erratic nature of their schedules, we often had to cancel our meeting times. They both hoped to pass the Educational Commission for Foreign Medical Graduates (ECFMG) exam, which would allow them to enter a residency or fellowship program in the United States. Dr. Saboortinat eventually succeeded, and the last time I heard from him, he had a residency at a hospital in New Jersey. They have both settled in the United States.

That first year, a large group of Volunteers gathered in Hamadan for Thanksgiving. The Birds kindly hosted us in their roomy home. We played touch tag football, swapped stories and sang favorite songs as someone strummed the guitar. This was my first contact with my fellow PCVs since the end of training, and it was good to see a few familiar faces. Many of the Volunteers, however, came from other groups and had already served a year or more. Most would be gone by spring.

During my three years as a Volunteer in Iran, I rarely took part in these gatherings, partly because of the distance and also because I kept remarkably busy with work and social life in Tuyserkan. Occasionally, I went to Tehran, but I did not like the city much. I would rather stay home. Another problem with those gatherings, which made me uncomfortable, was that often when a group gathered, especially if non-Volunteers were present, individuals would inevitably start telling funny stories at the expense of Iranians. Soon they were trying to outdo each other in this regard. Sometimes it turned into—perhaps unintentionally—Iranian bashing. Best to avoid that altogether, I thought.

I did become well acquainted with two Volunteers, whom I saw from time to time. John Metz, served in the town of Nahavand, which lay over the mountains to the south of Tuyserkan. He worked in agriculture, having grown up on a farm in Iowa, I believe. He told me a funny story about his experience with growing sugar beets. The idea was that he would plant a test area with improved seed, using the most up-to-date methods. In theory, his output would be so much better than what was used locally that the farmers would all eagerly switch to his methods. Unfortunately, it did not work out as expected. When harvest time came, John's sugar beets proved to be much smaller than the local average. Thereafter, when he went to the teahouse, someone would occasionally remind him of his sugar beet harvest, and everyone would laugh good-naturedly.

The other Volunteer, Neil Hart, worked in city planning in Hamadan. He was a trained city planner from San Francisco. He served three years at his post and often hosted holiday gatherings for his fellow Volunteers.

City planners often became frustrated because the Iranian government would bypass its own local experts and hire foreign consultants, paying them what seemed a small fortune. Apparently, Tehran assumed that if they cost so much more than the Peace Corps Volunteer, their advice must be that much better.

Neil came with Jack and Phyllis Bird to Tuyserkan early one summer, so that we could all hike over the mountains to Ganj-Nameh above Hamadan, a full day's march.[4] Along the way we saw many tribal groups already in their summer pastures. This was a memorable outing for us all.

Winter in Tuyserkan was relatively brief, usually from mid-December to late February, but temperatures could occasionally be frigid and snowfall plentiful. The snow did not last long in the town, but the mountains were covered for many months. I remember my first year watching the snow line gradually descend to the streets of Tuyserkan. At first, I noticed snow on the tops of surrounding mountains, a short while later the entire slopes would be covered, and then it would be snowing in town as well.

Snow and rain posed a particularly difficult problem for people who lived in flat-roofed adobe houses as most of us did. As the snow melted, the water would seep into the thick mud roofs, which often leaked and could collapse if not treated properly. On each roof was a heavy stone roller. After the homeowner or the *barfi* (snow-shoveler) had cleared the snow by scraping it into the yard or the adjoining kucheh, the roller would be passed again and again over the softened roof to press out the water and to firm up the ado-

---

[4] Site of Achaemenid rock inscriptions

be. Once when my roof was leaking, Turon threw handfuls of salt onto it and passed the roller over it a few times and the leaking stopped. These were amazingly effective treatments. One had to take great care when walking through the lanes after a heavy snow-fall for a pile of snow could come suddenly from a rooftop onto your head. *Barfi*s usually called out a warning, but sometimes it came too late.

After the snow came the rains of March and April, and that first year the rains were heavier than anyone could remember. This, too, posed a threat to the flat-roofed houses of the town. In my case, the eight-foot wall surrounding my courtyard became sodden and final-ly one night, when it could hold no more moisture, a section col-lapsed into the back yard. For several weeks, my private world was exposed to passersby, who could now see into my private world. This was a strange feeling, like sudden nakedness before the inquisi-tive eyes of strangers. Eventually, a new, brick wall replaced the old mud one.

May through September were the dry months when every day brought cloudless blue skies. Strangely, in Tuyserkan there was one exception. Each year on a single day in July, around the time when the grapes were being harvested, clouds would form over the moun-tain tops and late in the day a brief shower would fall. It was over as quickly as it came. Locals referred to it as "the rain that washes the grapes." I could never understand this phenomenon, and had I not witnessed it, I would have suspected a tall tale.

To survive those long, cold winter nights, Iranians had a won-derful device, the *korsi*. This was a square wooden table approxi-mately two feet in height and three feet on each side. Under this, a round *mangal* (brazier) of lighted coal was placed. Only *zoghal-e vezm* (hard coal) would do, and it had to be covered in ash to exude an even warmth. If the coals were not prepared by someone who knew their business, it was possible poisonous gases could be pro-duced. Over the table a *lahof* or large quilt was spread. Family members and guests shared the *korsi*—there was no central heat-ing—sitting on cushions with their backs resting against the wall and their lower bodies extended under the *lahof*. Sometimes it was a struggle not to doze off as the heat penetrated one's lower limbs. On top of the table, dishes of fruits and nuts and sweets were placed for guests, and constant glasses of tea were served. After guests had departed, family members stretched out under the *lahof* and slept contentedly until morning. Turon knew all the tricks to preparing a fine *korsi*.

In early 1968, several months before my arrival in Iran, Peace Corps evaluator Park Teter mentioned an encounter with my (future) *korsi* in his report,

> After crossing the snowy pass above Tuyserkan and trudging through the town's thawing alleys, we were glad to gather around Rick Sullivan's corsee [sic]. . .. As we swilled tea and nibbled snacks spread on the corsee, the shared warmth from the brazier spread luxuriously, inducing a drowsy undercurrent. . .. We had dinner around the corsee, and then beer and much talk. . . we slept under the common quilt. . .. Around the corsee breakfast and a morning and a lunch blurred together as if I had no itinerary.[5]

In winter when I visited the homes of friends for dinner, there was always a temptation to stay the night, but I usually resisted and headed home down the empty streets and *kuchehs*. Empty that is of humans, but I would inevitably run into packs of dogs. They frightened me. Iranians and dogs were constantly at war. In the daytime, the dogs withdrew to the gardens and would skulk away if encountered. At night they became bolder and roamed in packs, snarling as they picked through garbage along the muddy lanes. I had to pass them on my way home alone late at night. Sometimes they would fill the entire lane in front of me and stare in my direction with warning growls. Then, I would quietly retreat to find an alternate route to my door. One night I remember well, walking down the main street, which had a divider in the middle. Suddenly up the other side, trotting in the opposite direction, appeared a huge pack of dogs. Wherever they were bound, I was happy not to have attracted their attention. I should add that Iranians considered dogs to be *nejes* or ritually unclean. Any Muslim coming in contact with a dog would have to bathe to purify himself before prayer. Children

---

[5] Park Teter and Richard Wandschneider, "Overseas Evaluation, Iran, January 1-31, 1968," pp 1-2, Box 4, Program Evaluations, 1968-1969: Iran to Korea, Office of Evaluation, Record Group 490, Records of the Peace Corps, National Archives, College Park, MD. Jack Vaughn, then-director of the Peace Corps noted on the cover of the report: "This is a most provocative review [and] profound in parts. Even though it frightened me, I relished it."

often treated dogs abominably, kicking them, throwing stones. No one kept a dog as a pet. Only in the villages did shepherds keep dogs to guard their flocks. This was a sad relationship to witness, especially for a dog lover like me.

That first Christmas, I started a tradition of sorts, inviting friends and their families to a party in late December. I managed to find a tree and decorate it with cut out figures and chains of colored paper. I even had a homemade piñata, which was a great hit with everyone, young and old. I would blindfold one of the children and give them a stick to hit the piñata; if they were lucky, they would break it open. Inside were all kinds of candies. Sometimes, one of the fathers would insist on taking a turn with the stick. I continued these parties for the three years I was in town.

For my male friends, I would throw a New Year's Eve party, with appropriate food and drink. Around midnight, we would take the Christmas tree out into the courtyard and set it ablaze. I told them this was an old tradition in America. They seemed thoroughly to enjoy the evening, capped off with our favorite group musical exercise. Standing in a circle, we responded wildly to the command of the recording: *Harcheh, harcheh, zudtar, gheyr, gheyr, gheyr-e camar!* ("Rotate your hips as fast as you can!") These parties were a thank you for all the times I had been entertained at their various homes during the year.

Other gatherings were not tied to the calendar. That first spring, my friend Seyed Mahmud Emami bought a used car, a 1960 Ford. This was a big deal in Tuyserkan, where there were not many privately-owned vehicles. There is a delightful custom in Iran that when you make a major purchase, win the lottery, and so forth, you are obliged to provide entertainment or small gifts for your friends. In keeping with this tradition, he invited a number of us to ride to the top of the pass on a pleasant evening, and there we held a small party with singing and dancing and cakes and cookies and tea. When Hassan Rahmani, another teacher friend, won a small lottery, he, too, gave a party for all of us. This was a nice practice, I thought.

From my earliest days in Tuyserkan, I had been introduced to the occasional practice of smoking opium. It served to relax one after a heavy meal. In some homes, the *mangal* and the opium pipe would appear after dinner, and everyone would have a *poke* (puff). Sometimes the women also took part, depending on who was present. I never had a good sense of how common this practice was, but it was not rare in Tuyserkan.

I knew a few men who were addicted, and for the older ones, sixty years or more, the government issued permits to purchase a certain amount each month at the local pharmacy to maintain their habit. On the permit was a picture of an addict hanging by his neck from the chain of the pipe, not an attractive message. Nevertheless, it seemed a humane and sensible way to deal with the situation.

At one time or another I saw judges, police and even a doctor smoking opium at Gazandar Bala.   Addicts usually ate very tiny pieces of opium a few times a day. They did not smoke much because they could no longer satisfy their craving in that manner unless they smoked all day long. Friends told me that addicts were no fun because they no longer enjoyed occasionally sitting around the *mangal* and participating in the ritual that accompanied smoking.

Since my arrival, opium had become more plentiful because the government had recently decided to allow more poppies to be grown to supply morphine to the international and legal drug market. There were a number of fields around Tuyserkan. At harvest time a few soldiers took up positions in each field to make sure that the drug did not get into private hands through the black market, but inevitably some of it did.

Opium was the first stage of processing the raw sap. Each poppy pod was scraped by hand with a metal blade, and a sticky white sap would ooze from the wound. Workers would then come through the field and collect the sap, which would be rolled initially into what resembled a Tootsie Roll. This was sliced thinly and smoked or eaten in the case of addicts. Further processing and refining would produce heroin, which was far more potent and addictive. I never encountered this latter drug in Tuyserkan in those days.

When a group of friends smoked, one of them would often serve as the *saqi* (master of ceremonies), preparing the pipe and assisting the smoker. Opium pipes could be fancy in design with costly embellishments in silver work. The ceramic bowl at the end of the pipe, which actually resembled a dried poppy, had a small hole in the top. The small piece of opium would be stuck to the warmed bowl just behind the hole. Then, a lit coal would be carefully selected with tongs from the *mangal*. This was held just above the piece of opium. At the command, "*poof kon*," the smoker would blow through the wooden pipe making the coal glow and the opium bubble and turn into vapor, which the smoker would then inhale. After each *poke* the smoker (or *saqi*) would rearrange what was left of the opium, using a pin that was attached by a thin chain to the pipe. Gradually, the piece was totally consumed, and the pipe was handed to the next participant. Tea and sugar were served after smoking because the opium tasted rather bitter. The previous smoker would sit back quietly and enjoy the pleasurable feelings of the moment. Unlike other drugs, smoking opium did not bring about a frenzied reaction, but a serenity encouraging pleasant conversation. Iranians said of one who had smoked, *rafteh behesht* ("He has gone to heaven"). One had to take care not to smoke too much, otherwise it would rob him of sleep.

The residue that collected inside the bowl was called *shireh* and was much more potent than the original gum. Gradually, the bowl would fill up with this, and it would have to be scraped out.

During my Peace Corps years, I never encountered opium outside the Tuyserkan valley. When I visited Iran in 2003, I was invited to smoke at a gathering at a friend's house in Tehran, but I declined. The present regime has shown less toleration for this drug than did its predecessor. And yet addiction to this and other drugs seems to be a serious problem, especially among the young.

One of my most memorable experiences was when Terry O'Donnell visited Tuyserkan for the last time in July 1971. He stayed for five days, and what a busy time it was. He and I were invited to many different homes for lunches and dinners. For the first time, we had hours to talk as we walked in the gardens. Although his Persian vocabulary was limited, he understood a great deal about the people and the culture. He ended his stay with a final visit to Gazandar Bala, which he described here in his diary:

> We were in the end of it all Jim, Ehsani, Ehsani's two . . . boys, Nasrollah and a nice older man named Sayyid. . . .. Ehsani found a place for us down-stream. . . .. We crossed the meadow and then walked down an incline to a small terrace of turf above the river. There were young plane and poplar to either side of it and a vista of the river, a chain of pools ringed by big, gray boulders, a little fall between each pool.
> It was about dusk when they brought down a mangal from the teahouse. I had some opium with me, from Hamadan, but we ordered some Tuyserkhani [sic] stuff as well. Before, however we could get started, the food came; kebab, bread, onions, mast [yoghurt]. So, we ate first, and it was so good, the meat wrapped in the bread with the onion and then

dunked in the mast, washed down with Moleair [Malayer] arak.

After dinner we began the opium. It was smooth strong stuff and I had three *bas* [pieces], Nasrollah kindly holding the pipe for me. We hadn't gotten very far along when the thunder started, great boulders tumbling down the valley. It was very beautiful under the trees, the mottled, heavy sky, sometimes flashing yellow with the lightning. The rain came in great splats.

The rain never became all that heavy but we thought that it might and so we got up and went to stand under the trees, the two little boys huddling under the blanket, Nasrollah holding the coal for Jim. Sayyid and I talked. He told me that life, the goodness of life, was times and places such as these.

The rain stopped. We went back to the carpet. They brought another bottle of *arak*. We smoked a little more. The woods smelled so sweet from the rain. Finally, it was ten, perhaps eleven. It was getting late to get a car. The others went back to the teahouse to flag down a car. Jim and I stayed on for a while, talking. Then we went back as well. Jim taking my hand and helping me up the bank.

At the teahouse we sat on the porch bench waiting for a car. I was very happy what with the vodka, the opium, the night, a friend. But suddenly it occurred to me that I must have some memento of the night, partly because it had been such a good night, partly because I knew it was to be my last night in Tuyserkhan [sic] and for ever and ever, and partly because I knew that it probably would be the last of such nights in Persia for me.

The memento that occurred to me was a coal from the mangal from which we had been smoking the opium. I mentioned it to Jim, how sorry I was that I hadn't remembered to take a piece. He immediately got up and took the lantern and went back and got a lump of coal for me. I was grateful to him from the bottom of my heart.

A man they knew, a nice man, came along in his car and gave us a ride down to the maidan. . . .. I remained awake till dawn, breathing in the rain-fresh air which came through the French doors from the garden, lulled by the opium and thinking back on my last day and night in Tuyserkan."[6]

---

[6] Terry included this diary excerpt in a letter he sent to me on January 1, 1972. The original letter and the diary are in the archives of the University of Chicago.

My friends seemed to smoke more often that third year. I believe more opium had suddenly become available as a result of the new plantings in the area. Interestingly, Mansur and Dabaghi temporarily gave up smoking completely when Mansur became engaged to a young woman from Tehran. She was Dabaghi's close relative, and Mansur did not want any rumors circulating that might reflect badly on his character. This might put off his future in-laws. For the few younger men I knew who had become addicted, the situation was not pleasant. They spent a good deal of their time smoking and not always among friends and sometimes shirking family responsibilities.

Travels Near and Far

In early March 1969, a bus full of newly minted hajjis returned to Tuyserkan. They had made the pilgrimage to Mecca and now family and friends rushed to meet them as they slowly made their way to their homes. It took a long time for each of them to walk the short distance to their houses, for everyone wanted their blessing. People believed that these individuals brought with them a certain grace that for a short while could be imparted to those who welcomed them ceremonially. During this spiritual interlude, I noticed, much to my surprise, one hajji pulling back his coat-sleeves to reveal a half dozen or more expensive-looking wrist watches on each arm. Obviously, these had come into Iran, without paying custom duties, and their sale would go a long way toward covering the cost of the sacred journey. Here was a neat blending of religion and commerce, an age-old phenomenon common to all faiths.

Iranians also loved to celebrate the ancient pre-Islamic rituals of No Ruz, marking the beginning of the Persian new year at the vernal equinox (March 20). At home, a family set up a table prominently displayed with seven objects beginning with the letter "S," such as *sabze* (greens), *sumaq (sumac), samanu (*sweet pudding), *sirke (vinegar), seer* (garlic), *seeb* (apple), *senjed* (wild olive). They always included a mirror and a Qur'an, which showed an interesting blending of Islamic elements within a largely pre-Islamic ritual. Presents were exchanged and new clothes purchased. Schools closed for two weeks, and everyone, who could afford it, traveled to visit relatives or friends or just to see new places. At that time of the year, hotels in popular destinations were full to overflowing.

After that first hard winter, I set off for Abadan in the extreme southwestern corner of Iran with two friends and their families. Our destination was approximately four hundred miles away. We took the bus to Dorood, and there we boarded the train for Ahvaz. We traveled second class, and the seats were wooden benches, so no one slept much on that overnight trip. Still, everyone was excited as we moved slowly from the high plateau down to the broad flat plain that stretched all the way to the Persian Gulf. There had been substantial rainfall and this, added to the annual snowmelt from the mountains, had turned most of Khuzistan province into a great lake extending as far as the eye could see. All that remained above water was the rail line and villages built up on mounds along the way. It would be weeks before the turgid waters receded, and life could get back to normal.

In Abadan, site of the great oil refinery, we stayed at the home of Sayyid, a friend, who had worked many years for the oil company. He could remember the days under the Anglo-Iranian Oil Company, when British officials treated their Iranian workers shabbily, excluding them from housing and recreational areas reserved for Europeans. Now all that had changed. We spent several pleasant days as his guests before returning to Tuyserkan.

After we returned to classes in early April, not much new work was undertaken before the beginning of the final exam period in mid-May. My students' grades were on average lower than those in other classes. This occasionally became awkward, especially when a friend had a relative in one of my English classes. In one case, Dabaghi's nephew received a low grade, and Mansur told me plainly that I should have given him a higher mark. When Hajji's oldest son, Hushang, failed my class, his father was upset. Clearly, he thought I should have factored in our friendship when determining his son's grade.

In June, with all my teaching responsibilities over for the year, I set off alone on a three-week trip to northern Iran, traveling through Kurdistan, Azerbaijan and Gilan. In Khalkhal, I visited my friend, Jim Belcher. He was situated in a largely Azeri Turkish-speaking town, and not surprisingly, his Persian language skills had developed only slightly. He told me that although the government forbade the use of Turkish in class, all the Azeri teachers used it.

When I was with Jim and a fellow teacher, we visited a local site of pilgrimage just outside the town. It was a revered tree covered with multicolored ribbons, one tied on by each pilgrim. Each one of these sites across Iran—and there were many—had some special claim to miraculous power. It may have been the tomb of a local saint or a "holy" tree that was believed to grant wishes, for a child, a son, a cure, and so forth. Tuyserkan had at least one such site. Although orthodox Islam frowned on such superstitious practices, still, they went on.

My favorite stops on the trip were Ardebil and Astara each a stone's throw from the Soviet border. Recently, a volunteer had wandered innocently across the poorly marked border and had been arrested by Soviet border guards. This caused something of a crisis in Iranian-Soviet relations. When he was eventually released, he was immediately sent back to the United States. In the former city, I visited Kathie and Bill Kreager with whom I had trained. Later, I toured the magnificent shrine of Sheikh Safi al-Din built in the 16th century. The tile work and intricately carved wooden screen in the tomb-mosque complex surpassed anything I had seen elsewhere. From Ardebil the road drops precipitously several thousand feet to the shores of the Caspian Sea, which is well below sea level. In Astara everything seemed different. Houses had slanted, thatched roofs to handle the copious rainfall. Farmers grew rice and other humid-climate crops rather than the wheat, sorghum and cotton of the drier plateau. Large wetlands occupied the land behind the coast. The Caspian itself was not terribly exciting, a very salty body of water, not particularly refreshing to swim in. The beaches there were gravel rather than sand. Nevertheless, it provided a nice change of scenery. As impressive as anything I saw, was the dramatic climb from the coast to the plateau. The narrow road wound with many twists and turns toward the summit. Vegetation gradually thinned. On the north side of the mountains there was thick forest, once over the pass, however, vegetation suddenly became sparse. It was a world transformed in comparison to the narrow coastal lands far below.

I had no sooner returned to Tuyserkan, after a brief stop in Tehran, than I received a surprising and unannounced visit from my landlord's family. I had just finished showering when the doorbell rang. When I opened the door, there stood his wife and children, announcing that they planned to set up living quarters in the part of the house I was not using. I was shocked, but I managed to get them to leave. Dressing quickly, I raced to the Office of Education to explain my predicament. My landlord had come back to town without warning, they said. Obviously, by sending his family, he hoped to bypass all the red tape of the bureaucracy and present them with a fait accompli. His gambit succeeded. After some discussion, it seemed the only solution was for me to pack up and find another house.

Actually, the office helped me find other accommodation in a short time in a different part of town. The new situation was better. I moved to an older home made of adobe with some brick. There was a huge dirt courtyard at the front of the house with a few fruit trees but not much else. The house was much smaller than the previous one. The landlord promised to install a shower, which he eventually did after much prodding on my part; even then I had endless problems with it. The kitchen consisted of one small, dark room, which Turon considered a comedown from the large, bright one we had left behind. Situated across the narrow hallway were two medium-sized rooms, one for eating and entertaining and another for sleeping. These looked out on a small, tiled courtyard on the opposite side of which were a few steps leading up to a back entrance, opening onto a lane leading into the countryside. The WC was on the far side of the small courtyard near the outside door. Songbirds took up residence each spring in the open rafters, and some days their endless chirping drove me to distraction.

One considerable advantage was that the front door of the house opened directly onto a broad, dirt avenue leading up the hill to the center of town. No more *kucheh*-living for me. A downside was its location just a few doors from the entrance to Shahpur High School, where the student traffic flowed several times each day. This would be my home for the next two years (1969-1971). I paid 225 *tomans* ($30) per month rent.

That summer of 1969, Peace Corps Iran wanted to try a new method of in-country training. The incoming TEFLers would be divided into small groups of eight or so individuals, and each group would train for a month in a separate location. One group was coming to Tuyserkan, where they would do their teacher training, and Ehsani would direct that program. I would assist him. We also welcomed a former PCV, Alta Lu Townes, who had served in Shiraz and was a skilled teacher. In late July they came, staying at Hajji's hotel. They enjoyed the comfortable accommodation, and he was, of course, delighted to have the business.

The program ran very smoothly, and we encountered no serious problems. The Ehsanis went out of their way to make the group feel welcome. All of our trainees continued on to their assigned sites later in the summer.

I should mention an unusual issue that arose with one of the trainees in the Tuyserkan group. He was a Baha'i. Members of this denomination, which had originated in Iran in the mid-19ᵗʰ century and was an offshoot of Shi'a Islam, were considered heretics by many conservative Iranians, especially members of the *ulema* (Muslim scholars). Although the Pahlavi regime had taken a very tolerant position vis-à-vis this group, feelings could be quite hostile within the general population. Iranian Baha'is did not usually profess their religious affiliation openly, but one often heard rumors about certain leading politicians and businessmen. One of our language teachers had been a Baha'i, and he had apparently proselytized in villages near Kermanshah. That was a dangerous business.

Anyway, the Peace Corps, if they knew, did not inform Ehsani. When it came time to fill out the required police documents, a mini-crisis arose. One of the questions asked the religious affiliation of each trainee. If the trainee wrote that he was a Baha'i and someone noticed, his position in the classroom could well have become untenable. But neither could he be expected to write in the name of some more acceptable religious denomination. After some consultation with Ehsani, I suggested that George leave the line blank. It was more than likely no one would notice. These forms probably would be stuck in a drawer and never read. He took my advice, and that was the end of it. Later, he was assigned to Daran, but he found more rewarding service working in a school for the blind in nearby Isfahan.

Volunteers generally had a break after a year of service, a time when they could travel abroad. To the west, Iraq was closed to us because relations with the United States had been severed following the 1967 Arab-Israeli War. I had originally planned to visit India, I had even obtained my Indian visa, but that trip fell apart when my proposed travel companion changed his mind. Fortunately, at the last minute, my good friends, Jim and Mary King, invited me to join them on their travels to Greece, Cyprus, Israel and the West Bank. Jim came from a Greek-American family, and he naturally had great interest in Greek culture.

We left in late August, flying to Athens. This whole region was on the so-called Hippie Trail in the 1960s. Thousands of young Europeans, Americans, Australians and New Zealanders made their way along the Mediterranean and then overland through Turkey, Iran, Afghanistan, Pakistan to India and Nepal, or in the opposite direction. One could travel very cheaply in all these countries. The lure for some was transcendental meditation made famous by the visit of the Beatles to an Indian ashram early in 1968, for others it was cheap and plentiful drugs, such as hashish. For many, it was both. Unfortunately, many of these young Westerners had little interest in the cultural surroundings through which they traveled, and when they grouped together, they produced a microcosm of the very society from which they hoped to escape. Local populations avoided contact whenever possible.

From our base in Athens, the three of us traveled to a number of Greek islands, Crete, Rhodes, Kos. To my later embarrassment, I was relatively uninformed about the political situation under the Junta (1967-1974) and the difficult conditions facing many Greeks at that time. We met up with Jim's mother and aunt for part of our stay. With them, we visited the Valley of the Butterflies near Lindos on the island of Rhodes. Travel was easy and relaxing, and I did not have to worry about maintaining a certain image as I did when I was in Tuyserkan, and all eyes were on me.

From Greece we traveled to Cyprus and that was an eye-opener. Although our visit coincided with a period of relative calm in relations between the Greek and Turkish communities on the island, we could sense the underlying tensions. Our service in the Peace Corps did not guarantee that we were well informed about political and social conditions in the countries on our itinerary. Although I had a vague sense of what we might encounter in Israel, only two years after the Six Day War and the occupation of the West Bank, Gaza, and the Golan Heights, nothing had prepared me for the realities of Cyprus. Fresh from golden beaches and carefree days on several Greek islands, we arrived in Nicosia expecting more of the same.

We headed to Paphos, an ancient city at the western end of the island, near the spot where Aphrodite, according to Greek mythology, sprang fully formed from the sea foam. On the way, we passed through the British Sovereign Base of Akrotiri, allotted to London in the negotiations that created an independent Republic of Cyprus in 1960. What a contrast to the surrounding parched landscape, for it was late summer. We passed through long stretches of green grass and carefully manicured playing fields, flower beds and trees and neat bungalows, stretching along the roadside. It seemed so unreal, as if a piece of England had dropped from the sky. Traveling on a Greek-Cypriot bus, I noticed that whenever we passed through a Turkish-Cypriot enclave, only sullen faces stared up at the bus. At one point I saw, with some amazement, the long barrel of a dug-in, camouflaged artillery piece, pointing in our direction from a near-by hillside. No sooner had we arrived at our destination and checked into the hotel than several plainclothes detectives, Greek Cypriots, visited us, wanting to check our passports and asking why we had come to Paphos, which was not then a common tourist destination. A short time later we strolled into the center of the city and recognized a number of blue UN sentry boxes strung out along the top of an ancient wall. The wall, we were told, separated the Turkish-Cypriot enclave from the surrounding Greek-Cypriot sector of the city. The UN contingent included a small marching band, which played at sunset, as I recall, but it could not do much to lift the sense of tension that we felt. When we departed the island after several days, it was with a feeling of relief that we headed to Tel Aviv.

In those days, the Israelis were "sexy," having vanquished the combined Arab forces in a stunning victory in the June War. Many young Americans flocked to the eastern Mediterranean land to contribute their efforts, usually working on a kibbutz. I, too, shared the mythology of the time, regarding a feisty people who had won against all odds and made the desert bloom on the heels of Arab indolence and mismanagement. I remember standing on the West Bank side of the Dead Sea and watching Israeli warplanes attack supposed guerrilla positions on the Jordanian side, as great plumes of smoke rose high into the air. Conditions on Cyprus seemed to me much worse than those between the Mediterranean and the Jordan River.

After several weeks of travel, I was quite happy to board the Iran Air jet for the return trip to Tehran. With American encouragement, the shah had established good relations with Israel. In addition to regular commercial flights between Tehran and Tel Aviv, he supplied Iranian oil in return for Israeli expertise especially in agriculture and military training.

It had been a pleasant holiday, but I was ready to get back to familiar places. I was eager to show my slides to my Iranian friends. I had taken care to film historic buildings and coastal scenes, without any passersby finding their way into my images. I was quite proud of that achievement. As I showed slide after slide to the Ehsanis, Mr. Ehsani finally asked, in mock seriousness, "weren't there any people where you traveled?" Everyone burst out laughing, and I was forced to join in. I learned an important lesson.

My friends were likely more interested in the local inhabitants than in historical relics and pristine landscapes.

During the summer, Sally Chaffee, a new Peace Corps Volunteer, had been assigned to teach in the girl's high school (Parvin Etesami). She was to have her own rooms upstairs in the home of a conservative family, the Bahramis. Hajj Bahrami held a position in the Office of Education.

Sally grew close to the family, especially to their daughter, Azar. As she recalls, she had breakfast with them every morning.

> They didn't want me to be *tanha*, afraid I'd be lonely. Sipping tea with the sugar between my teeth and those special mornings with boiled stomach wrapped in sangak. And most dinners at night. Three or four of us washing clothes in the *hayat* [courtyard] with those little cardboard boxes of Tide. I thought I had mastered the technique, but the other women would always, good-naturedly, redo whatever I washed. And tea parties - to me very funny, unlike Western social gatherings, the more women wearing the same dress under their chadoors, the better. It showed their shared good taste, I guess.[7]

They were good to Sally, but she often felt restricted, knowing that they expected her to adapt to the local mores. Most Iranians had difficulty understanding how American parents could allow their daughters to live on their own in foreign lands, without any guidance or supervision. Although Sally conformed to local expectations in many ways, it was a challenging situation from the start.

We spent a good deal of time together during her two years' service, and the assumption was that we were having sexual relations. Nothing I said could convince friends otherwise, so, I finally gave up trying. Whether or not the Peace Corps should assign single women to sites in Iran had been argued over repeatedly. I do not recall the Peace Corps asking my opinion about assigning Sally to Tuyserkan. Would she have been happier in a larger city, I wonder? It was a great burden for her, a fact that I did not fully appreciate at the time.

Barbara Johnson who had served in Tuyserkan had actually left early, at Christmas 1967, finding life too confining and lonely. "I lived on the second floor of a home of a respected, conservative

---

[7] Sally Chaffee, e-mail message to author, June 21, 2020.

family, presumably for my protection," she recalled. "My own socializing involved occasional dinners at the homes of my students or
others who made the effort to be kind to a foreigner, and of course
the Ehsanis, who made me feel very welcome. I loved them all!
My Farsi really developed in Tuyserkan; I was proud of that."[8]

Sally received little support from the high school administrators. She was pretty much on her own in that regard. The young
female students often acted up in her classes, and she had no figure
comparable to Mr. Ehsani or Mr. Dabaghi to whom she could turn.

Fortunately, the Ehsani family gave her a lot of support. The
two of us often were guests in one home or another of that extended
family. But I was definitely freer to move about town and interact
with friends and colleagues.

Sometimes we went to Hamadan together for Thanksgiving or
just to visit the volunteers there. We planned the annual Christmas
parties together and worked to decorate my house. We had one party for the Ehsani family and friends and another for the Bahramis.
Sally visited Tehran more often than I did and with good reason, I
think.

That first No Ruz, we traveled together to southern Iran. We
had a fine holiday, visiting Isfahan, Shiraz, Yazd, Kerman, Bam,
Bandar Abbas and the island of Qeshm. There was, of course, always the awkwardness of traveling with a young woman who was
not my wife. Iranians would assume we were married and if we
said we were not, that would only confirm their belief in the sexual
licentiousness of young Americans and other Westerners.

This situation led us into a trap of our own making. On the bus
from Isfahan to Shiraz, I entered into a long and amiable conversation with a fellow passenger. A middle-aged Iranian from Shiraz,
he told us all about his family—he had several children—and he
seemed genuinely pleased to talk with us. We did not say that we
were married, but we allowed him to come to that conclusion. After
all it did not matter, for once we had arrived in Shiraz, we would
say our farewells and probably never see him again. We did not
want him leaping to other conclusions. As it happened, however,
we had not booked a hotel, and we arrived quite late in the city. All
the hotels were full. Our new friend insisted, as only an Iranian can,
that we spend the night at his home; he would be proud to have us
stay in his large guest room, he said. It was impossible to wiggle

---

[8] Barbara Auerbach, e-mail message to author, July 12, 2020.

out of his invitation, try as we might. And we could not suddenly announce that we were not Mr. and Mrs. Goode. So, we gave in, feeling rather guilty about our deception. We slept well despite the situation for we were exhausted from the long trip. We left early the next morning following breakfast with our host.

The rest of the trip was less stressful. We joined up with several other Volunteers in Bandar Abbas and took a dhow to the island of Qeshm or Hormoz just off the coast. We spent the day walking around parts of the island and viewing remains of the old fort that the Portuguese had taken control of in 1515. Back in Bandar Abbas, we visited the fish market held on the beach. Here, many women covered their faces with a black mask as well as their bodies with a chador. This was an unusual sight in Iran for on the plateau, where most Iranians lived, women rarely covered their faces in this manner. It was a characteristic shared by traditional peoples around the shores of the Gulf.

By the time we returned to Tuyserkan in late March, it was only a few months before my tour of duty would end. For some time, I had been considering volunteering for a third year. I was unprepared to leave my Iranian friends and the town for which I had developed such strong attachments. I was just beginning to understand how everything functioned. After almost two years in Tuyserkan, I had come to realize that I was learning far more from Iranians than I could ever teach them. This was a common discovery for Peace Corps Volunteers everywhere. In my case, I had learned to appreciate the present more, to be less focused on what would happen next. I also valued friendship more than ever before.

In addition, I had taught an exceptionally good group of English students for two years, and if I stayed, I could take them through a third year of instruction and help to strengthen their language skills; this seemed a particularly important reason to stay. I would also be in town for Sally's second year, and my presence might lend some support. I was in no hurry to leave and had no particular agenda to pursue in the United States. The Peace Corps was happy to have me stay an additional year, and the Ministry of Education agreed.

Mr. Ehsani, however, was soon packing his bags in preparation for his trip to London. He had been chosen to receive a British Council fellowship, which would allow him a nine-month stay in England, where he would study English among other subjects. By early July, he was gone. Leaving his family and his new-born daughter, Mahtab, was no easy decision. Iranians have a few well-known sayings about good friends who are absent, "*Ja-esh khali ast*" (His place is empty) or "*Ja-esh sabz shod*" (Grass has grown in his place). In the coming school year, I would miss him more than I could have guessed.

I began to make my own plans for home leave. I planned to fly to Dublin for a short rendezvous with a former Iran PCV. On the way back, I would stop in London for a few days to visit Mr. Ehsani. Those two stops would take up about a week of my holiday. After Ireland I would head for Boston and the Cape for a reunion with family and friends. I did not plan to return to Iran until mid-September.

In Dublin I met up with Gerry Bennett, who as a Peace Corps Volunteer had worked as a secretary at the Peace Corps office in Tehran. An Irish-American Catholic, she wanted to experience life in the Republic of Ireland when her tour ended. So, there she was, working in a raincoat factory, earning IR25 pounds a week. I stayed at a bed and breakfast she recommended in one of the seaside suburbs. I was apparently the only paying guest at the time. Each morning I came down to face, all on my own, an impressive selection of meats, pies, breads, rolls, eggs and so forth. I could never do it justice. One night Gerry took me to an Irish pub, and when late in the evening the band played the Irish national anthem over and over, frenzied patrons danced on the table tops. It reminded me of tipsy Southerners at the playing of "Dixie," which I had witnessed often in Virginia and Washington, D. C.

Next stop, Boston and Cape Cod. The few weeks at home went by in a flash. My parents had separated long before; my mother lived in Florida, and my father worked long hours. My older brother was serving in the army in Vietnam. Thus, I spent most of my time with my sister and her young family. Her husband was serving in the US Air Force in Thailand, and she was pleased to have another adult in the house.

One day we hosted Sally's father, who had driven down for the day from his home in Upstate New York. Naturally, he was concerned about his eldest daughter. She had been a great help to him after his wife's early death. I assured him that she was doing okay, and I agreed to take a few items for her back with me.

On another occasion, some good friends from college visited. I was pleased to see them and their children again, but I always felt that they did not really understand why I had entered the Peace

Corps and now, why I had chosen to stay a third year. Nevertheless, it was sad to say goodbye to them once again.

It seemed strange to be back in the United States. It was obviously so different from Iran, especially now that the antipathy toward the Vietnam War had spread widely among the population and seemed the topic of everyone's conversation. Very few were interested in my own experiences in the Middle East. At most, they listened politely as I tried to convey what a remarkable country and culture I had encountered. I imagine I had changed more than I knew. I was soon looking forward to leaving again and heading back to Tehran.

In London, I enjoyed seeing my Iranian friend again, but his situation was not pleasant. He told me that the English were very cold and unfriendly toward him—of course, he was comparing them to the folks in Salt Lake City! His only acquaintances were other foreigners in similar situations. His landlady only spoke to him when the rent was due. A doctor had prescribed so many aspirin tablets for a stomach complaint that he had suffered medical complications. He would stay the full time, but I noticed when he returned the following year, his English had barely improved.

And then back to Tehran and my third year in Tuyserkan. It would prove more eventful than I could have imagined. After my time in the United States, I felt certain I had made the right decision.

The Final Year

Although 70 percent of Iranians still lived in villages in 1970, I did not visit any of those around Tuyserkan until my final year. I seemed to keep fully occupied in the town itself and surrounding gardens. That fall, however, I made two trips to different villages. In late September, we had an invitation to dinner in Farisfaj, not far from Tuyserkan. We stayed the night. It was a traditional pottery village, and I enjoyed walking around the workshop and examining the pots set out to dry in the sun. Many of them were low-fired *ollahs* used for drinking water, but there were also large, glazed jugs for storing *torshi*.

Early in October we went to a wedding in Karkhane, a small village quite far from town. It was a very pretty place, with a river running through it and many trees. There were bands of traditional instruments, drums, flutes, and so forth. Men and women danced separately in long lines through the *kuchehs*. The music went on late into the night. A special shelter on poles had been built under which all the attendees were served dinner. There was a lot of good food, especially grilled meats, including lamb, goat and chicken. Our host set us off by ourselves—as befitted our higher status, having come from the city. I suppose in return we added to his standing in the community because we had accepted his invitation. We enjoyed vodka with the meal and opium after it. I watched men playing *Qaab*, a traditional game, in which three knucklebones were tossed into the air and wagers were won or lost depending on how the bones landed.   I had never seen this before. Mansur got angry with me because I insisted on seeing everything and taking pictures, and he thought, I imagine, that I should have remained more aloof from the activities of the villagers.

In spite of their humble status, villagers seemed to satisfy a few important needs in Pahlavi Iran in addition to tilling the land. Whenever there were commemorations in Tuyserkan of some historical event, such as the fiftieth anniversary of Reza Shah's coup d'etat (February 21, 1971) or the signing of the 1973 OPEC oil agreement, they made up most of the small crowd. The musical instruments were the same as those I had heard at the village wedding. Some official would have arranged for their presence in town. Yet, the formal addresses on such occasions used sophisticated language; I doubt many of the peasant attendees could have understood precisely what the speaker was saying. Peasants also made up most of the military's annual levy of eleven hundred young men from the district. I remember seeing them being farewelled by their families and loaded onto buses in the town square.[9]

On the way back the next day from the wedding, we stopped at two more villages. In one, another wedding was underway, and long rows of men and women were dancing in a sort of two-step shuffle. They were very graceful, and it was exciting to watch. The movements and the music reminded me of Native American cultures. City folk generally thought such activities only fit for peasants, having themselves abandoned such practices.

The second village was small and seemingly impoverished. I saw no trees, and water appeared to be in short supply. This was before the age of bottled water, but I had a raging thirst, so one of the village boys brought me a glass of murky-looking water. Although I should have known better, I drank it. Meanwhile, my com-

---

[9] Reportedly, the oil agreement would bring an increase of 12 million tomans a day to Iran.

panions bought two small carpets there, and then we headed back to town.

In the third week of October, I began to have severe headaches, and I was unable to eat any solid food for about a week. Then, I became jaundiced. The Iranian doctor called it *yaraghaan*. I decided to take myself into Tehran just to make sure everything was okay.

I felt fine when I arrived and even treated myself to a big meal at the Caravansary restaurant at the embassy. When I appeared at the Peace Corps office the next morning, however, the doctor reckoned that I had infectious hepatitis and immediately placed me in the Armish-Maag Hospital, usually reserved for US military personnel stationed in Iran. I stayed there for about two weeks. I decided that most likely the glass of water I had drunk in the dusty village back in early October had caused the illness. I remember seeing particles floating in the glass that was handed to me. I drank it anyway, lulled by the thought that after more than two years in-country, I could withstand the local microbes. I was very wrong. Interestingly, none of my Iranian friends had drunk any water in that village, only me.

The Peace Corps nurse was one of my early visitors. She came around Halloween and observed that I looked, appropriately enough, the color of a pumpkin. Thankfully, she did not say, "I told you so."

I arrived back in Tuyserkan in the third week of November. I had missed a month of classes. Students and staff gave me a warm welcome. I quickly got my classes back on track.

The new principal at Emir Kebir was no Ehsani. He seemed a weak character, overly impressed with his new position. Neither the students nor the teachers had much respect for Mr. Ashrafi-Zadeh. When I first received my teaching schedule from the Office of Education, it had been loaded with large, first-year classes. I complained strongly, and they agreed to make some changes and give me additional second-year classes. I had hoped that Mr. Dabaghi would be keeping an eye on this while I was in the States, but apparently, he had not.

Now, Mr. Ashrafi-Zadeh proved to be even more foolish than I had suspected. He did not believe that I had been sick but rather that I was just using that as an excuse to stay in Tehran. The two Mansurs were having a dispute with him, and he knew I was close to both of them. Perhaps, his criticism of me had been his way of getting at them. There was much more to come.

Once again, Sally and I went to the Peace Corps gathering for Thanksgiving in Hamadan. Mansur came with us. The weather had turned cold, and in the evenings we all gathered under the *korsi* at Neil's house, singing and telling stories. We had a lot of fun.

The following week I had to return to Tehran for a blood test. On the way in, I had a very unusual travel experience. Every Iranian bus had a *shawgerd-e chauffeur* or a young man, who assisted the driver in myriad ways. He bargained with and collected the fares from passengers, who hailed the bus along the road. He brought water to the passengers, kept the bus clean, took required paperwork into the gendarmerie posts along the way, and performed a hundred other tasks large and small. For his part, the driver was like the captain of a ship, to be obeyed without question. Usually, the relationship between driver and student was harmonious; the driver was the boss, and the assistant accepted his orders uncomplainingly.

On this singular occasion, as the bus wound its way up the icy road that led out of the valley, I suddenly became aware of loud voices at the front of the bus. The driver and his assistant were having a serious argument. The young man would not be silent, and the driver became more and more agitated. Finally, just before we had reached the crest of the pass, the driver had had enough. He slammed on the brakes, turned off the motor, and exited the packed bus, exclaiming for all to hear that he could take this insubordination no longer and that he was walking back to town. He started marching down the slippery road. There we were, left to our own devices on that bitterly cold morning. In an instant, the passengers rose as one and hurriedly exited the bus. They began to pursue the driver down the slope, pleading with him to come back and drive them to Tehran. What a sight! They used every argument imaginable. Soon, he began to weaken. He agreed to return, but only if the assistant said not another word and sat at the back of the bus for the remainder of the trip. The passengers promised this would happen. Then the group returned with the driver, dispatched the young man to the rear seat, and swore him to silence. Then, with a chorus of prayers, the bus started off again toward the distant capital. It was truly a remarkable experience. I did not dare to ask what had caused the argument in the first place; I feared starting trouble all over again.

My third winter in Tuyserkan turned out to be the coldest yet. It began with heavy rains, which soaked the wires leading into the house so that the lights flickered on and off for days. Then came the heavy snow and the cold, this all before Christmas.

Sally and I worked hard to prepare for the two Christmas parties, baking in the little tin oven and making decorations. On the day of the first party, Turon went off to the *hammam* to be clean for our holiday, she said. Everyone seemed to enjoy themselves. Later in the week, we invited Mr. Alghaws and his family to dinner.

Then, I gave my usual guys-only party for ten friends on New Year's Eve. This was an all-night affair. I went to bed as the sun was rising, but Mansur and several of the others went off to one of the villages for the day. They had amazing stamina. Sally, meanwhile, had gone to Tehran to celebrate and to say goodbye to Neil and John, who were heading back to the States via the eastern route through Asia. After all the partying, I was broke and had to borrow money from Farhang, a shopkeeper friend. I made a New Year's resolution to watch my expenses more carefully, so I would have money for the No Ruz holiday.

Farhang was my only close friend with a background different from the others. He had little formal education. He owned a dry goods shop in the main street, selling soaps, cooking oil, dried food items, buttons and thread, cigarettes and matches, and so forth. I cannot remember how I first came to know him; I probably sought refuge in his shop one day from a pack of young boys harassing me with "HELLO MEESTER!"

One of my frequent complaints was the behavior of young boys in the streets. Sometimes, when I passed them on my own, they would bellow out "Hello, Meester!" repeatedly, which annoyed me a great deal. Or they would make rude comments. I wanted them to show me the same respect they would a local teacher. But, as long as I lived in Tuyserkan, this situation did not improve. Only rarely would a passing adult reprimand them. In towns where I was a stranger, sometimes children would throw small stones if I wandered into neighborhoods off the beaten path. This happened in Malayer (and later in Turkey also). I wondered what they might have heard their parents or others saying about the *kharaji* (foreigner).

Anyway, I often spent time in Farhang's shop talking with him, drinking glasses of tea and making small talk with his customers. It became one of my regular *patuq* (hangouts). Perhaps, I was good for business. In age, he was somewhere between thirty and fifty years old, probably closer to the lower number. It was often hard to tell someone's age in Iran because men and women seemed to age so quickly once into their twenties. I never knew whether this was a result of climate, diet or some combination of factors. He was a devout Muslim, who always seemed quite happy to see me when I turned up. Once or twice, we walked together in the hills above the town. He had a wife and children; I never met his wife. I felt comfortable enough asking him for this short-term loan, and he quickly agreed. Mansur tried to discourage me from fraternizing with Farhang because he said he was uneducated and from an inferior social class. In this case, I did not take Mansur's advice.

It was from the vantage point of Farhang's shop that I first had a good look at the local *darvish*, who frequented that part of town and often appeared at the shop door. He was a mystic, choosing poverty to move nearer to God. He never begged, but pious folk gave freely, for many considered him a holy man. Farhang would routinely give him a few *rials*, and in return he would recite a short blessing and move on. He dressed in an extraordinary fashion with a long cloak and a tall conical hat. He carried a calabash to collect alms and a small ceremonial steel axe. Later, I bought a painting in the Tehran bazaar, which reminded me of this memorable figure.

Manuchehr Solemani's shop became another hangout. Manuchehr was a member of our gang; I do not remember how he was connected or to whom, but he often seemed to be present at our frequent gatherings. His shop was located on the street leading up to the high school, and I often stopped in at the end of the day on my way home. He bought and sold bulk quantities of almonds and walnuts and dried fruits such as *senjed* (wild olive) and apricots and *kashk* (dried yoghurt). What fascinated me most was his constant use of the abacus in his business dealings. I had seen pictures of these in books discussed as some medieval calculating instrument, which I assumed had disappeared centuries earlier. And here was Manuchehr, on any given day, clicking the various rows of round wooden disks to make all kinds of complicated transactions. I was impressed. I never took the time to learn how to use the abacus, but I bought a beautiful handmade one in the local bazaar.

I tended to get very melancholy at holiday time. This became more of a problem than ever as 1970 faded into 1971, because I was trying to decide what path I should follow in the coming year after leaving the Peace Corps. I considered going back to graduate school, traveling in Europe, teaching English in Japan or teaching at Alam High School in Mashhad in eastern Iran. A number of ex-PCVs had chosen this final option, including the Kings, and it seemed to be working well for them. I went around and around with each of these options, as gradually Mashhad moved into first place.

In early January a new English teacher, Masudi, arrived in Tuyserkan. He was a relative of one of the school administrators. When I first met him, he observed that American English was what villagers spoke and that British English was far advanced compared to what was spoken in the United States. The Office of Education decided to take two of my classes and one of Sally's to fill out his schedule. This upset me a great deal. One of the classes to be reassigned was the third-year class I had especially enjoyed teaching. I briefly considered leaving. Then, as if on cue, Mr. Valizadeh, the assistant to the Minister of Education, arrived in town. He was like a king holding court; everyone showed him respect. He had studied in the United States and spoke English well.

Mansur insisted on taking our case to him, and I agreed although reluctantly. I feared whatever happened, there would be hard feelings. He heard our story ably presented by Mansur, and then he questioned the new chief of education. Finally, he told the chief that he had made a mistake, and he was not to take any of our classes. We were, after all, guests in Iran, who voluntarily offered our assistance to teach local students.

The whole situation had obviously become an embarrassment for the local officials. I had mixed feelings about the outcome. On the one hand, the new English teacher was an Iranian who perhaps should have taken precedence, on the other hand, I had decided to stay an additional year, in no small part because I wanted to teach the third-year English class. Mansur had put himself in a difficult position vis-à-vis the chief of education, and I worried that there might be retribution. Nevertheless, my schedule stayed as it had been. I kept the third-year class.

A week or so later, the chief called me into his office and warned me not to get involved with the "band of friends," by which he meant Mansur and some of his fellow teachers. He said they had ulterior motives of which I was unaware and that I should keep my distance from them. I knew they had filed a complaint against the chief with the Minister of Education. Forty-one teachers had signed the document. He would be gone by the end of the school year.

This was the year for formal visitations. Not long after Mr. Valizadeh's visit, a group of important government officials came to town. Known as the "Eyes and Ears of the Shah," an ancient Iranian administrative device, these half-dozen men, all of whom had retired from important ministerial posts, spent several days in Tuyserkan, inspecting the functioning of various government agencies. They also received petitions and complaints from ordinary citizens; apparently, they had the authority to make on-the-spot decisions. All of these men had studied abroad and spoke English well. I attended one of their public sessions and was impressed at how smoothly they seemed to carry out their duties. I wondered what impact their reports would have in Tehran.

Shortly after these events, Mike Jerald, a Peace Corps field officer, paid a visit, bringing with him Professor Lipson from Harvard University's School of Education. He startled me with his comment that he did not think there was much difference between Iranian and American teachers and students. I did not agree. He observed three of my classes, which he complimented. The Peace Corps was developing yet another program for a new group of TEFLers in summer 1971, and they asked me to join the staff. I could not give them a firm answer immediately because my plans were still indefinite. The program they were developing would run through early September.

Mansur had other more important matters to consider that winter, his upcoming marriage being at the top of the list. His bride to be and her parents visited Tuyserkan to meet Mansur's parents and family members. Mansur fretted about all the expenses he was incurring. His future in-laws had spent a lot of money for the couple, and they obviously expected him to do his part. He told me they wanted him to buy diamonds for his fiancé.

Early in February, I had a second medical emergency. A blister had opened on my small toe and became infected. The toe swelled and became extremely painful. After several days, I could not walk, and the infection had spread to my lower leg. At first, I had hobbled to and from the schools to teach, but for the last few days the foot was so painful that I had to stay home, crawling to the door if anyone came to visit. Dr. Yazdon-Bakhsh prescribed a thick black ointment that looked and smelled like tar, which he said would open the wound and allow it to drain. After a few days, it worked. Then, he cleaned the area and packed the deep hole left in my toe with penicillin and placed a wick to facilitate drainage. The whole experience lasted just over a week.

As my third year in Tuyserkan was slowly coming to an end, my draft board surprised me with a 1-A classification, placing me, I thought, in the most eligible category for the draft. I was then twenty-six years old and supposedly beyond draft age. I wrote to Roger Wangsness, who handled such administrative details for volunteers in the Tehran office. He replied promptly, saying that I should not worry; this was only a formality. I would have this classification until age thirty-five.

In 1971 the mourning month of Muharram started well before No Ruz. Muharram is arguably more important to Shiites than even the fasting month of Ramadhan. The tenth of Muharram, *Ashura*, is surely the most important day for this is when the martyrdom of Imam Hussein at Karbala (681 CE) is commemorated, with passion plays (*Taziyah*) and somber marches of pious men dressed in black, chanting as they move in long lines through the streets of towns across the country.   Traditionally, these devout folks would carry lengths of chain or long blunt knives with which to flagellate themselves as they marched along, resulting in bruises and bloody gashes on their upper bodies. The shah's government had forbidden these more excessive behaviors, and the police were on alert to see that proceedings did not get out of hand.

This was the first year I had been in Tuyserkan for Ashura. I kept a low profile, not wishing to offend anyone. I could observe long lines of penitents moving through the lane outside my courtyard door. I heard them chanting repeatedly as they passed by, *Karbala imshab, Karbala* ("Karbala tonight") and *Ya, Hussein*! (Oh, Hussein!) There were perhaps five hundred men and boys in the group I saw. Men from each quarter of the city paraded through all the other quarters throughout the evening each trying to outdo the other in its fervor. They carried black flags and illuminated pictures of Imam Hussein. I marveled anew at the power of religious belief.

I saw people weeping in the street, Turon among them. My housekeeper believed implicitly in the supernatural. She once told me a story about a casual acquaintance of mine, who had overdosed on opium and was as good as gone. His father was a mullah, and he prayed over his son for hours. Eventually, the young man vomited up the opium and came back from the dead. It was all due to the intervention of his father, she said. Mullahs could do all sorts of things.

I attended a *rowza* (mourning ceremony) in a private home and also was invited to the mosque to watch different groups perform. I rarely visited a mosque in Iran unless it had been opened specifically as a tourist/historical site by the government. But as I had been invited by the imam, and I would attend with friends, I decided it would be okay to go. Iranians could be extremely sensitive about non-Shiites entering their mosques, and I did not want to offend. The population in Tuyserkan was wholly Shiite, and I remember one day there was a buzz in the bazaar when a visiting Sunni Muslim had prayed in the main mosque. One could tell from the gestures during prayer whether an individual was Sunni or Shiite. Anyway, that was a big deal to the local folk. In later years, I was surprised to find that Sunni congregations throughout the Middle East welcomed visitors to their mosques; only very sacred sites of pilgrimage were off limits. This was quite different from my experience in Iran.

During Muharram, my next-door neighbor, Hajj Mohmeny died at age fifty-five. His appendix burst, after he had complained of stomach pain for four or five days. A doctor had misdiagnosed his symptoms. His son, Mehdi, was a good friend, and I visited him with other friends to express our condolences.

For a nice change, that No Ruz, the Peace Corps offered volunteers a Persian reading and writing program in Mashhad. This was a good opportunity for although I spoke Persian fluently, I could read and write the language only at an elementary level. Besides, I had not visited Mashhad previously, and there was also the possibility of a trip to Herat in Afghanistan at the end of the program.

Mashhad was the most important pilgrimage site in Iran; it possessed the tomb of the Eighth Imam, Reza, who had died in 818 CE. A magnificent mosque had been constructed near his shrine by Goharshad, wife of Timurid emperor Shahrukh in the early 15th century. Successive rulers had added to the splendor of the complex. Shah Abbas (1587-1628) had made a famous pilgrimage across the desert on foot to solidify the importance of this site for all Iranian Shiites.

In mid-March I headed for Tehran where I filled out some of the paperwork for termination. Then I took a twenty-six-hour bus trip to Mashhad. What a trial that was but well worth the effort. The reading and writing program was excellent. Mr. Naraghi, one of the instructors from Tehran, praised my pronunciation, but he said that I needed to expand my vocabulary. One day he suggested that I go with him to the shrine, assuring me that if anyone objected my Persian was good enough to silence them. Still, I declined. I also met a volunteer couple, John and Joan Meyer, and we spent a lot of time together during the program and later in Herat. After my pleasant experience in Mashhad, I decided that I would sign a contract to teach at Alam High School in the fall.

Entering Afghanistan seemed like stepping into the past. I saw virtually no private cars in Herat. The food was different from that in Iran, more of a spicy, South Asian influence. Clothing, too, was much more traditional. Men dressed in baggy trousers and loose, flowing shirts; many wore turbans. Few women were seen in public at all, but if they did appear, they wore the *chadri*, which covered the entire body. There were no modern stores and most of the goods in the shops had been imported. Horse-drawn carriages or *droshkies* provided most of the transportation. We stayed about a mile outside the city center in a hotel built by the Soviets. The broad dirt road leading into town was lined on both sides with tall pine trees. What an experience to ride in a carriage at night along this thoroughfare, no lights and the only sounds being the clip-clop of horses' hooves and the wind blowing in the pines. Drugs such as hashish were cheap and plentiful in the country, and this attracted the hippy crowd. I supposed that fifty years earlier Iran had been much like Afghanistan at the present time.

On my way back through Tehran, I told the Peace Corps that I would work on the training staff in Hamadan that summer from June 1 until early September. The pay would be $125.00 per week plus room and board. That was about three times what I made as a volunteer ($150.00 a month, $75 paid in Iran, $75 put in a stateside bank account).

I also saw Terry O'Donnell again. He was about to set off for Muscat to do a story for *National Geographic*. He had been trying to get there for six years, and now with the change of rulers, he had obtained a visa.[10]

Back in Tuyserkan, Sally and I received an invitation to have lunch with a Mr. Keani, who was the Majlis candidate for Tuyserkan of the ruling Iran Novin Party. This meant that he would likely win the parliamentary seat. He had spent ten years in the United

---

[10] Sultan Qaboos had replaced his father in an almost bloodless coup in July 1970. He then set about opening the sultanate for visits by outsiders like Terry.

States; his wife was American. At lunch he told us about all his ideas to bring change to the area. He hoped he could convince the Peace Corps to send several specialist volunteers to the district. He said he could guarantee me a good salary if I decided to stay in town the following year. He was full of enthusiasm, but he faced considerable challenges, I thought.   At one point, he referred to some of the locals as "animals," which was not a good start.

Mike Jerald came to town with John Giordano, who would head the training program that summer. John had previously served as a volunteer in Libya. He visited a few of my classes and did not provide a lot of feedback except to say that I should use less translation in the classroom. "It might be a long summer," I thought.

By the end of my third year in Tuyserkan, I was having doubts about the overall benefit of the TEFL program.   Most of my students would probably have learned as much from an Iranian teacher. To expect more was probably unrealistic. And yet, I had just agreed to help prepare an incoming group of English teachers.

I had been really pleased, of course, with the progress of my third-year class. Seyed Mahmud's eldest son, Hushang, proved to be one of the best. I would miss them.

As usual, classes ended with a whimper, not a bang. Fewer and fewer students would turn up for classes as the exam period approached, and one day the principal would declare the school year officially at an end. You could not squeeze in one more lesson. This usually happened sometime in early May.

That spring 1971, stories began to filter in from Tehran that university students had been protesting all the money that was being spent to commemorate the 2500th anniversary of the Iranian monarchy. Police had apparently reacted with harsh measures; there had been shootings and many arrests. I wondered if these disturbances would spread beyond the capital.

Before my exams began, I paid another visit to the Bashiri family in Ghasr-e Shirin. I did enjoy spending time with them, although I did not find their frontier town particularly interesting. We drove out to the Khosravi border post where one could often buy goods that had escaped customs duties, items like tea, cigarettes, knives, cigarette lighters. On the trip back, we passed many tribal groups with their flocks, heading north to summer pastures.

When I returned to Tuyserkan, I borrowed three hundred *tomans* from my friend, Gomawr, to tide me over until I got my next Peace Corps pay. Gomawr was a *dendun-saz*. He made false teeth for those who could not afford to go to a trained dentist in Hamadan or Tehran. He must have learned his trade through an apprenticeship. He seemed to have many customers, mainly villagers, whenever I visited his office. I enjoyed his company; he was a thoughtful man. I saw him near the end of my service, shortly after the unexpected death of his father-in-law. He seemed depressed at the thought that he had now become responsible for the welfare of his wife's numerous young siblings.

As a farewell gesture, Hajji invited Sally, Mansur and me to dinner at the hotel. It was a very pleasant evening. I had spent much time over the past three years in his establishment, and I would surely miss the place.

I went to Tehran in late May to continue the termination process. I stayed several days and dined out with friends at some of the eateries that I especially enjoyed, Xanadu, the Hotel Naderi and Ray's Pizza. While shopping one day in the Supermarket, I ran into an acquaintance from my class at Georgetown University. I saw him from a distance but could not quite place him. He recognized me, however, and we soon were recollecting tales from our days in the School of Foreign Service. I invited him to a party that evening at a friend's house. He came, but I never saw him again after that night.

He was in Iran working for a major agribusiness company that had signed contracts to set up large-scale farms in Khuzistan province in southwestern Iran. These would grow export crops such as cotton. Many small farms in the region would be amalgamated into large concerns that would use heavy farm equipment imported from abroad. This was all part of the government's development plan, but it did not bode well, I thought, for the peasant farmers, who would either become poorly paid laborers on these huge farms or more likely join the flow of rural folk, who had abandoned the countryside and headed for Tehran. This development upset me a good deal. Here I was, I thought, working hard to make a small positive contribution and to try to understand the culture, and establish personal relationships, and this company comes in knowing next to nothing about the place and proposes to turn local society upside down.

I returned to Tuyserkan at the end of May with two obligations, to give a farewell party for my friends and to finish packing my belongings. The party was easily accomplished. There were seventeen men with whom I had associated closely over the previous three years. This would be the last social event with them at my house. They presented me with a Tuyserkan carpet as a parting gift. We had tasty food, chicken and lamb kebabs, salads, mast with dill, immature almonds and walnuts soaked in salted water, melons and grapes, and drinks both hard and soft. Soon the spirit moved one friend after another to recite well-known verses or to sing a favorite song, or to get up and perform a dance in the circle, snapping his fingers to create a rhythm. The merriment lasted until sunrise, when in pairs and threesomes they said their goodbyes and left. When the last of them had departed, I fell into bed.

When I awoke, the packing remained. Such a sad time. And then to make things worse, Turon arrived in floods of tears over my leaving. I spoke to the doctor about employing her after I left, and he seemed interested. I hoped that would work out. She had done her work well and having her to rely on had made a great contribution to the quality of my life there. Later, I learned that a new Peace Corps couple had been assigned to Tuyserkan, so perhaps Turon would continue working for volunteers after all.

Oh, how I would miss this little green valley. I did not look forward to the hustle and bustle of a big city. It was fortunate that I would be spending the summer in nearby Hamadan, so I would be able to come back from time to time during the next several months. This was not a final good-bye.

I arrived back in Tehran just in time to farewell Sally and her traveling companion, who were heading west through Turkey along the Black Sea coast. I wondered how she would remember her two years in Tuyserkan. I know she carried with her a special fondness for the Bahrami family.

I stayed at the Polaris Hotel, a two-star establishment that had been welcoming Peace Corps Volunteers from the beginning. It did not have much to recommend it, except that it was centrally located, within easy walking distance of the US embassy and the Peace Corps office, and it was cheap. There was a bar in the basement complete with barmaids, who tried to entice customers to buy expensive drinks that contained little alcohol. More than one unsuspecting volunteer had ended the evening with a tab that easily equaled his month's salary. Or, as in my case, a full-blown argument and refusal to pay the outrageous sum. It was a business that preyed on lonely volunteers and one to be avoided.

I spent the first week of June finalizing my termination. On June 6, my volunteer service came to an end. I moved into the more upscale Atlantic Hotel at Peace Corps expense, waiting for the start of the summer training program.

I had time during those relatively idle days to reflect on my years in Tuyserkan and to ponder what I might have achieved. Regarding teaching, the most I could claim is that I had worked with much determination to provide my students with basic English language skills. Progress here for many had been limited, but some few had prospered. Hopefully, this would assist them in their later studies. At the least, students would have experienced a quite different method of teaching compared to what they usually encountered. Perhaps, that would be of some future benefit.

And I developed lasting friendships. Above all, I came to understand a great deal about Iranian culture, which is not readily apparent to outside observers. This knowledge would influence my judgments ever afterwards in my research and teaching. My international interests first nurtured in the Peace Corps would lead me to pursue a career in scholarship focused on the Middle East. The Peace Corps experience had changed my life, although I did not immediately understand the significance.

Peace Corps Group 19 departing for Iran, June 1968 (back row 1st on right, Jim and Mary King, Author, 6th from right. Jim Belcher, 2nd row, 3rd from left)

Winding mountain road into Tuyserkan valley

Hajji (far left) with his family in front
of Hotel Alvand

Ehsani children, (l. to r.) Masoud,
Saeed and their cousin, Minoo,
playing in stream at Gazandar Bala

Turon making lunch in kitchen of my
first house, 1969

Doshanbe and Abibi Ehsani

Ehsani, Mahvash and the children
in the gardens above Tuyserkan

Director of Education for Hamadan province (2ⁿᵈ from right)
visits my classroom

Mr. Alghaws with his buffalo at his
village of Goegtapeh, summer 1969

Seyed and his brother, my nextdoor
neighbors, shoveling snow off
their flat roof, 1969

Main square in Tuyserkan, winter, 1969

Ehsani, Bashiri, Daboghi (l. to r.) at a
gathering at my house, 1969

Hassan Rahmani dancing in a circle
of friends at my house, 1968. Mansur
and Mashollah Ehsani on left

Field of opium poppies outside
Tuyserkan, showing slashes made to
obtain gum

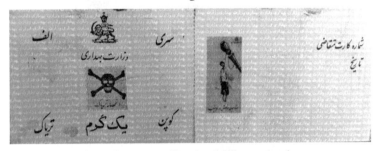

Government issued coupon, allowing addict to purchase one gram
of opium at the pharmacy, 1969

At Gazandar Bala with (l. to r.) Dabaghi, Terry
O'Donnell, Author, and Nasrollah Ehsani, 1969

Group of Peace Corps trainees, staff, and family, celebrating end of training at Hotel Alvand, summer 1969. Seated (r. to l.) Mahvash Ehsani, Ashraf Bashiri, Ruth Cathcart, and Alta Townes. Standing, (r. to l.) Author, Ehsani, Pat Cathcart, George McDonald, Chuck Howard, Abdullah Eghtedari, and Nick Montalto

(l. to r.) Sally Chaffee, Mansur
Ehsani, Fathi and Turon, 1970

Turon, Fathi and Author at
Christmas party, 1970

Village men dancing during
wedding in Karkhane, fall 1970

2

Together in Mashhad, 1971-1973

Courtship

John Giordano, our program director, arrived a few days after I checked into the Atlantic Hotel. John had served in the Peace Corps in Libya, 1966-1968, and stayed on there to supervise teachers in the field. Then came the Gaddafi revolution in 1969 and John's reluctant departure. After he completed a TESOL degree at the University of Minnesota, he contracted with Peace Corps Iran to direct their summer TEFL programs. John had many creative ideas about teaching, and I remember in particular his emphasis on "teacher presence," being self-aware in the classroom. He could be intense at times, and I recall he chewed us all out early in the program because he thought we had given less than our complete attention to a visiting speaker. Despite a rocky start, John and I became good friends over that summer and beyond.

One of his novel ideas was to hire a small group of native English speakers to spend several hours with us each day for a week at the Atlantic Hotel. They would be our guinea pigs, and we would try out on them the different teaching methods we would be using to instruct the new Volunteers when they arrived in country. This group of expatriates from Australia, England, and India would provide feedback, allowing us to sharpen our teaching skills.

His directions to the ten expatriates must have seemed bizarre; they probably had never experienced such group interactions. Nevertheless, they went along with the program for which they each received US$35 at the end of the week.

One participant, Virginia Dixon, a young Australian, made this poignant observation in a letter to her parents,

> Every morning we have one hour's lecture on the teach-
> ing of writing, grammar, and so forth. Then TEACHER

PRESENCE, in which we do all sorts of strange cha-
rades and experiments. Actually, I must admit some of
it I am quite enjoying, but you come out feeling wrung
out emotionally as they demand that you have a reaction
to everything—I guess this is called GETTING TO
KNOW ONE'S SELF AND HOW YOU APPEAR TO
OTHERS!! Everything is in capitals . . . We had one
dreadful experiment today, when we all had to sit round
in a circle and hold the person's hand next to you then
with your other hand express to him or her a feeling.[1]

On the last day of the program, I invited Virginia (Ginny) to
dinner at the Hotel Naderi. We spent a wonderful evening getting to
know each other. This was the first time I had been able to talk with
her alone at any length.

Ginny had arrived in Tehran in March at No Ruz. She had accepted an invitation from the Australian ambassador, Barry Hall and
his wife Diana (Di), old family friends, to live with them until the
end of the year and provide companionship for their nine-year old
daughter, Libby, whenever they had to go out for social occasions.
Libby was alone, for her three older brothers were all at boarding
school in Australia.

Earlier, in spring 1967, Ginny had traveled overland from
Bombay to London on an Indiaman camping tour. Like many
young Aussies and Kiwis, she had planned to spend time abroad in
what was then a fairly common maturing process. Although her
time in the Middle East had passed quickly, she was excited by the
sights and experiences in the region and hoped to return one day.

She had come back to Australia from England in 1969 and was
working in Canberra when the Halls offered her this position. She
accepted, thinking that this would give her an opportunity to learn
more about Iran, its culture and people. She understood that living
with a family, even in a large residence, would require some adjustment on her part. She had lived on her own or with roommates
for almost a decade. But she was adventurous—as her week with
the Peace Corps would suggest—so why not go to Iran.

Her life in Tehran was unlike anything she had experienced before. She befriended other nannies in the capital, volunteered at the
library of the British Council, worked briefly for a travel company

---

[1] Letter dated, June 22, 1971. Ginny's parents saved all her letters from
abroad and returned them to her when we left Australia in August 1978.

called Iran Safaris, and took long hikes with friends out into the beautiful countryside above Tajrish, the northern suburb where the residence was located. She even began to teach a dance class for young girls at Libby's school. She became friends with Teresa Huntley, the social secretary of the British ambassador, and enjoyed a day-long excursion with them to the holy city of Qom. She was invited to lunch at the British embassy with Sir William Luce and his entourage. Luce was in Tehran to meet with the shah to discuss ownership of several islands in the Persian Gulf. The Halls supported a number of charities, and Ginny helped out at the residence when there were special events scheduled. There were also frequent large gatherings of a diplomatic nature. At one of these, Ginny was seated next to a prince of the former Qajar dynasty, a Farman-farmaian. When he discovered that he had been seated next to a nanny, he turned his plate upside down in protest.

To her chagrin, however, she was not having any personal contact with Iranians on a day-to-day basis. This, it appears, was the common experience of much of the foreign community in Tehran. Members moved in a narrow circle of fellow countrymen and expatriate acquaintances. Any Iranians one encountered were likely servants, drivers, or government officials.

After our evening together, we knew that we wanted to see each other again, but the new Volunteers had arrived, and I was leaving for Hamadan early the next morning. The remainder of the training would take place in that distant city. Thus, we had to be creative. Over the next two-and-a-half months, we got together a total of six times. She came to Hamadan three times, I traveled to Tehran twice, and once we went together to Isfahan with several of the program staff. Other than letters, telegrams provided the easiest means of keeping in touch, but they were often delayed. Sometimes Ginny would receive one announcing my imminent arrival, but she did not know whether it referred to my past visit or an upcoming one.

When she and her friend, Sue Dillon, another nanny, came in early July, John and I let them have our room at the Bu Ali Hotel. (Our group had stayed at the same hotel in 1968.) We had a good time, visiting the many sites in the city. I also introduced Ginny to Terry O'Donnell, whom she liked as much as I did. We ate dinner in the hotel garden, or we went up to Ganj-Nameh, a favorite spot, where there were many open-air cafes along the river. Although our time together was limited, we had some wonderful experiences that summer.

Later, when I visited Tehran in mid-August, we had a last dinner with Terry before his departure for the States. I knew he was having great difficulty separating himself from Iran, where he had lived since the 1950s. He wondered what lay ahead for him in Portland, Oregon, his hometown. That night we dined at the Xanadu, one of our favorite restaurants. Terry came dressed in a white dinner jacket and treated us to a number of stories about his adventures over the years in Iran. He was a great storyteller, and we so enjoyed listening to him. Years later he would publish a marvelous account of these adventures titled, *Garden of the Brave in War* (1980). When I read it, I was moved to tears. I can still remember his farewell that night. He put us in a taxi, then turned in the opposite direction, walking slowly down the kucheh toward the darkness. We watched him disappear into the night.

We did not see him again for over twenty years, although we corresponded regularly. I often regret that we did not meet again until summer 1993, after more than a score of years had passed. This was a sad reflection on how busy our lives had become.

Terry had eventually made a successful transition in Portland, working at the historical society and authoring a number of well-received books on the history of Oregon. When we finally visited him, we were accompanied by our two sons, Matthew and Zachary, then ages seventeen and sixteen, respectively. They enjoyed his company as he did theirs.

Our last visit with Terry—only Ginny and me this time—came in March 1998. He divided his time then between his apartment in Portland and his cottage at the mouth of the Columbia River, which he named "Crank's Roost." We stayed with him there, reminiscing about the old days in Iran and lamenting the sad state of US relations with the Islamic Republic. He could never quite understand, I think, how his beloved Iran had become the scene of so much brutality.

While we were there, he asked me to select an item from his Iranian artifacts, which I would receive when he died. His unusual request surprised me, but I did as he wished, choosing a *qibla* indicator, an instrument used to determine the direction of Mecca for prayer. Three years later, I received a package from his estate, which included the item along with a letter reporting his recent death. How sad, I felt, that I had not even known of my good friend's passing until many months after he had died.

Much later, I deposited his letters to me from the years, 1972-2000, at the archives of his alma mater, the University of Chicago, which holds his diaries as well. He wrote masterful letters. Anyone who wishes to take the full measure of the man should read that correspondence.

That summer of 1971 held many more adventures for Ginny and me. When she came again in late July, we went to Tuyserkan, so I could introduce her to my friends. We stayed at the Hotel Alvand, but we dined with families in their homes. Mr. Ehsani had returned from England so there was much to celebrate. Ginny had never visited an Iranian home, so she found everything new and unusual. Although she was excited, the situation was tiring for her as well. Wherever we went, she became the center of the women's attention. She enjoyed it all, but happily returned after a few days to the relative serenity of Hamadan.

I also met Richard Sullivan at Mansur's house that summer. He had come back to Iran for a visit as many former Volunteers often did, and he was happy that Mansur had married. Unfortunately, I did not take the time to talk with him then about his Tuyserkan experience, which I wish I had done. We never saw each other again. He died early in the new millennium.

At the end of August Ginny came back one last time before the program in Hamadan ended. After that, I would be heading to Mashhad to take up my teaching duties at Alam High School. We had talked in general terms about marriage but had made no decisions. In the days before her arrival, I thought a lot about what marriage would mean, especially if we stayed in Iran indefinitely. I knew I had come to love her and wanted her to be my wife. I did not want to wait any longer, and I hoped she felt the same.

The second day of her visit, at sunset, we climbed the hill of the ancient stone lion, *Sang-e Shir*. Tradition held that this ancient monument bestowed luck on young women about to marry. What a romantic spot, mountains in the background and the city below. When I asked Ginny to marry me, I took her by surprise. She was not expecting that question so soon. Her thinking, however, had obviously been moving in the same direction, for she quickly accepted my proposal. How happy we were that night. Later, we returned to the Bu Ali to share our good news.

After the Hamadan program ended, I spent a few days in Tehran, and we made some basic plans for our wedding on January 20. It was then that we called Ginny's parents in Australia from the main telephone exchange at the central post office. I used that opportunity to ask formally for their daughter's hand, which was still the practice Down Under. They warmly agreed. Ginny told them how much we would miss them at our wedding. Neither of our families would be able to make the long trip to Tehran.

Finding someone to marry us proved quite a problem. Neither of us was particularly devout, but in order for the government to recognize our wedding, and guarantee Ginny a residence permit, we had to have a church wedding. Two Protestant ministers and one elderly Catholic priest turned us down, and we were running out of options. Then Di came to the rescue. She said she had heard of a new, young Irish priest at St. Abraham's, Father Ambrose O'Farrell, who rode around Tehran on a motorcycle. Perhaps, we should approach him, she suggested. Being so much younger, he might be less rigid regarding whom he would marry in the church. We took her advice, and he quickly agreed as long as Ginny, an Anglican, agreed to meet with him for a few discussions before the wedding.

We decided early on to have two wedding receptions, one for expatriates, the other for Iranian friends. I thought my Tuyserkani friends would be more comfortable that way. Thus, planning for the separate celebrations went on throughout the fall. Most of the arranging fell to Ginny, as I set off for my new job in Mashhad on September 10, and only returned to Tehran once before the wedding.

Big City Challenges

I had opted for the teaching job in Mashhad because I knew I could not just hop on a plane in Tehran and say goodbye to Iran, perhaps forever. I had become so completely immersed in life in Tuyserkan over the past three years that I would have to distance myself gradually from that precious world. A sudden departure, I knew, would cause too much distress. Better this gradual distancing, with the pleasant thought that I could return to my idyllic valley from time to time over the coming months.

After my three years in tiny Tuyserkan, settling down in a large provincial city took some adjustment. Mashhad was an attractive center in those days, with a population of approximately five hundred thousand. It was the second largest city in Iran. Beyond the very crowded shrine area, where most of the pilgrims gathered, one could find broad avenues lined with huge poplar trees radiating from *meydans* (circles) full of flowers and statuary. Along one of these, Kuh Sangi Boulevard, lay the campus of Alam High School, which was administered by the University of Mashhad. It bore the family name of the shah's most influential advisor, Asadollah Alam, who served as both prime minister (1962-1964) and, later, Minister of Court (1967-1977). Alam came from nearby Birjand, a small town in Khorasan province. I am not certain how this institution came to be, but it was unique in Iran. Students were chosen by exam from all over the province; they all attended on scholarships. It was coeducational. When I taught there, 1971-1973, almost all the classes were in English, even science classes. The twelve foreign teachers in my first year, all Americans, had served in the Peace Corps, several in Iran and the others in Afghanistan, India, and Ethiopia.

I was excited at the prospect of teaching world history, but it proved a challenge. I did not have access to some of the basic materials of instruction such as maps, colored slides and supporting texts. I asked Ginny if she could find some maps and reference books in the Tehran bookstores and send them out to Mashhad.

I taught large classes, but the level of English ability among the students was quite remarkable. I had struggled in Tuyserkan to get the students to carry on a simple conversation. Here at Alam, some of the students spoke with near fluency and with an American accent. The students could commit reams of material to memory and reproduce it almost word for word on exams. Such memorization characterized much of traditional learning in Iran. What proved more challenging for them—as for students everywhere—was to respond to open-ended questions when they had to apply reasoning to produce their individual responses. They struggled also with writing a research paper. We spent time together in the Iran-America Society (IAS) and British Council libraries, both of which had decent history collections, but the results were often disappointing.

I soon learned that many of the students were unhappy studying history; they wanted more science classes. In another history class taught by a colleague, students refused to take the first exam. I did not encounter that particular problem, but it was always a struggle to convince them of the value of studying history. During my second year at Alam, the administration reduced the hours devoted to history, and I began to teach more English classes. A new principal had been appointed, Dr. Ehmad, who held a PhD in chemistry from the States. Perhaps, he was more sympathetic to the students' point of view. I know also that the Persian language instructors were complaining that their students should be devoting more time to the study of their own language and consequently less to the English language. As time went on, the number of class hours in English declined, and with it the language skills of the students. But all that happened after I had left Alam.

The students could be amazingly creative. Alam had an active student theater group, for example. We went to several of their presentations. One that we particularly remembered took place at the Science Faculty theater at the university and had political overtones. (Students from Alam had open access to university facilities.) Ginny had had a lot of training in classical dance, so I quote her diary here,

> The pantomime-dance was especially good, one boy dancing, completely untrained, to varying drumbeats, and it was beautifully done and extremely moving. It is amazing how much freer these kids are with their movements than we are. We would have had to be trained in dancing to perform like he did. Actually, it was a really surprising topic—very revolutionary—and everyone was amazed that they were allowed to put it on.

The students enjoyed administering little shocks to their foreign teachers from time to time. They might decide to walk out of class or not come at all. In another case, we had gathered all the history students together for a rare viewing of an English documentary on World War II. We had a few English visitors at the session as well. Whenever Hitler appeared, the students cheered. I never understood why they did this. Was it to shock us, knowing how we looked upon the Third Reich? Or did they really see the Fuhrer as in some way a hero?

Only in hindsight, did I begin to understand their reaction. An Iranian view of the war, a time when their country had been invaded by the USSR and England, joined later by the United States, and forced into the war against its will, would look quite different than our own. Why should the students accept the classical Western interpretation of the conflict? At the time, however, I was shocked.

One might reasonably have asked, I suppose, whether it was appropriate for an American to teach Iranian students world history at all. Maybe someone in the school administration did question this arrangement. Surely, there were cultural biases that I would have unintentionally tried to pass on to my students. None of this, of course, did I understand at the time.

Actually, I did have one memorable experience when I was teaching the period of the Persian wars against the Greek city states led by Athens. To my mind, this heroic event had always appeared as a centerpiece in the development of Western civilization. Looking at the same event from the heart of what had been the Persian empire, however, it looked quite different. From that vantage point, I could see small, almost insignificant disturbances on the far periphery of an otherwise mighty and illustrious empire. I recalled the adage, "Where you stand determines what you see."

During my two years at Alam, I did not become well acquainted with any of the students I taught there. Firstly, I brought with me from Tuyserkan conservative ideas about the proper relationship between student and teacher. These were very traditional. One should maintain distance from students, never fraternize with them. More importantly perhaps, for most of my time in Mashhad I was married, and Ginny and I spent much of the time getting to know each other. Some of my unmarried colleagues, however, spent a good deal of time with certain of their students and some of those friendships lasted well beyond Alam.

Finding housing turned out to be more of a problem than I had expected. When I first arrived in early September, the hotels were full as pilgrimage season was in high gear. Thus, I accepted the offer of Carter Bryant to stay at his house. I ended up living there for almost three months.

I was fortunate that Carter and his wife, Judy, were willing to have me as a guest for that length of time. I lived in the *zirzameen* or half cellar under the house and tried not to trouble them. They were an interesting couple, whom I got to know quite well during my extended stay. They had both served as Volunteers in Iran, Carter in Torbat-e Jam, 1966-1969, halfway between Mashhad and the border with Afghanistan, and Judy in Bam, 1966-1969, in the southeast, where my friends the Kings had been posted. Carter and Judy had trained together in Austin, Texas, and experienced the mass shooting on the University of Texas campus on August 1, 1966, that killed fourteen people including a trainee from their group. After their Peace Corps service, they married in the States following a whirlwind courtship, when Carter was on a brief home leave from his position as director of the Iran-America Society in Mashhad. They seemed like total opposites, Judy quiet, contemplative, Carter always a dynamo, racing around with a hundred tasks to complete, never far from a crisis. Judy was in her final months of pregnancy that fall, so she hardly left the house.

Carter knew everyone in the expatriate community. I valued his friendship; he would do anything for a friend. Sometimes I think people took advantage of him. He had many good ideas about changes he wanted to make at the IAS, but he faced opposition from the board. It was a rather stodgy institution. When he decided to hire native speakers to teach some of the advanced classes, the Iranian instructors nearly rebelled. I became one of those teachers, doing part-time work at Carter's request.

The Carter household was always a hive of activity, people coming and going constantly. There, I first met Andre Singer and Brian Street, two British anthropologist friends, who were carrying out research in the region. Our paths would cross repeatedly in subsequent years. They spent considerable time in Afghanistan, but Brian also rented a room in a house in the village of Zoshk, about forty kilometers west of Mashhad, where he was carrying out a study of local village society.

One happy experience came at the end of November, just after the first heavy snowfall. In the middle of the night, Judy went into labor, and when Carter tried to start the car, the engine would not turn over. He roused the five of us staying there at the time, and we pushed his car out the gate, down the snow-filled kucheh to the nearest street. There, he jump-started the car, and off they went to the hospital. Sean Bryant arrived a few hours later. Carter handed out cigars.

When Ginny visited in mid-November, she came with her good friend Julia, who had recently married an American, and she and her husband, Mike, were slowly making their way back to Australia. After a few days in Mashhad, they left for Herat. We continued the serious business of renting a house. This involved a few long sessions at the real estate office with the agent, the owner and several onlookers, who seemed to be cheerleaders for a successful outcome. We did eventually reach agreement and sign the contract.

As much as I had appreciated the loan of the *zirzameen*, I was pleased to be in my own place at the beginning of December. Ginny had stayed with me at Carter's when she came in mid-November. At Christmas we would be in our own home.

I had found a traditional style house in a good area of the city, actually within walking distance of Alam. The owner, Mr. Ghaffurian, who owned a small sock-knitting factory near the shrine, needed to do some work on it before I could move in. Most importantly, he agreed to put in a shower, but this could not happen overnight. Until that was completed, I went to the public baths. These were well designed, but it became increasingly difficult to go there in the evening as the fall temperatures dropped. I did not bathe every day. When Ginny came to visit in mid-November and again at Christmastime, we visited the baths together. We got steamy warm there and then raced the several blocks home, trying not to cool off too much until we could climb under the korsi. Early in the new year, our own shower came into operation, and we no longer had to make those nighttime journeys.

The house had a large courtyard surrounded on all sides by a high wall. At the front there was a shallow pool surrounded by several apple and cherry trees. Narrow flower beds ran the length of the courtyard. A slightly deeper pool in the back courtyard was used for washing clothes. In typical style, the WC was separated from the house in the rear corner of the compound. The house itself had four rooms. To the right as you entered the broad hallway, stood a large bedroom looking out on the garden. This room had tall windows that almost reached the floor and wide, tiled windowsills. The two small adjoining rooms to the left, separated by glass doors, served as a study and a sitting room. The broad hallway turned to the left and at the end stood the kitchen and beyond that what would become the shower room. It was quite large enough for us.

As for furnishings, I had purchased, sight unseen, the contents of Jim and Mary King's house, including a large bed, dishes, and other necessities. They had spent the previous year teaching in Mashhad, and I gladly arranged to buy what they would not take with them when they left. I brought only a few items with me from Tuyserkan, the korsi, which I had inherited, and some inexpensive floor coverings.

At the Christmas and New Year holidays that year, there were parties organized by the Iran America Society and by the British Council. We attended midnight mass at the small Catholic church. The congregation that night consisted of eight English-speaking expatriates and a group of French nuns, who worked at the leprosarium outside Mashhad.   The service was half in English, half in French.

During those early months, I became very aware of the pervasiveness of drugs in Mashhad. I was housesitting for a friend, when there was a loud knocking on the metal door, which opened onto the kucheh. I crossed the courtyard and opened the gate. In stepped an Afghan traveler in traditional dress. Afghans were a common sight in the city for the Hazara minority were Shia Muslims like most of the Iranians, and they often came on pilgrimage to the shrine. He was carrying something wrapped in a piece of cloth. When he unwrapped it, I saw to my amazement a huge cake of hashish, weighing perhaps a kilo and a half with a gold star stamped at its center. I had never seen so much of the drug in one piece. Assuming it belonged to my absent host, I explained that he was away and took delivery myself. The courier departed immediately. I left the hashish—unsampled—on his kitchen table with a note.

Much of the drugs, especially hashish, entered Iran from Afghanistan, where it was plentiful. Iranians seldom used it, preferring opium, but Westerners heading back to Europe on the overland route often carried some hashish with them. Sometimes they brought—or tried to bring—large amounts hidden in their luggage or in the chassis of their automobile. This seemed to be more than required for personal use and the assumption was that they planned to sell this cache at considerable profit when they got to their destination. Sometimes, they would hire a mechanic in Herat or Qandahar to hide the drug, and then they would set out for the Iranian border post at Taybad. Border police became experts at finding this forbidden import. Rumor had it that the individual who was paid to hide the hashish often tipped off the authorities once his customer had departed. Those apprehended routinely claimed that someone else had hidden it in their car or luggage. (Ginny always sat with our luggage at the border, just in case.) Whatever the truth, there were approximately eighty young foreign men languishing in the Mashhad jail. Their wives or companions, often with children in tow, found cheap accommodation nearby, waiting for trials or hoping for an amnesty. This latter seemed entirely possible in fall 1971, when the shah was celebrating the 2500th anniversary of the Iranian monarchy.

We all got caught up in these celebrations in one way or another. Most of our students, of course, thought it was a waste of money that could be better spent for the welfare of the people. Some Iranians seemed pleased with the attention their country was attracting in the West as a result of the elaborate commemoration. Many heads of state would be traveling to Persepolis for the festivities.

Fortunately for me, most schools closed for a week, so I was able to visit Ginny. When I arrived in Tehran everything was *shuluq* (confusion), gridlock traffic especially on Pahlavi Street leading from downtown to the northern suburbs. I sat in traffic in a taxi with the meter running. Finally, I could sit still no longer; I paid the driver and set out on foot.

During those few days, we got a lot of wedding details settled. One day we visited Mr. Ehsani at his office in the Ministry of Education, where he was awaiting a new posting. He agreed that two separate receptions would work better than one. So that was final.

I had an unusual experience at a government health clinic, where I had to go for a blood test and examination to make sure I did not have a venereal disease. Stripped down to my underwear, I stood in line with about twenty-five other grooms-to-be, waiting to be inspected. The doctor determined that everything was in proper order. Intended brides were not subjected to such scrutiny for it was assumed they were all chaste.

We also met with Mr. Avedissian, an Armenian-Iranian marriage registrar. He took responsibility for officially recording Christian weddings, Armenian, Assyrian, Protestant, and Roman Catholic. I do not know how many such registrars were at work in the capital. He explained to us what the government required regarding witnesses and documentation and what his fee would be.

While we scurried around the city trying to get as much done as possible, the Halls had arrived in Shiraz for the great celebration in the presence of the shah and the empress. They witnessed all the pomp and grandeur up close; all that we saw came via TV. The government had erected a magnificent tent city at the foot of Persepolis, the ancient Achaemenid capital of Cyrus the Great (560-530 BCE) and his successors. Here, the heads of state would spend several days socializing, feasting, and being entertained. Ambassadors and humbler folk stayed forty kilometers away in Shiraz hotels. They were bussed to and fro each day. Perhaps the most impressive event of the celebrations was a parade representing soldiers from each of the dynasties throughout Iran's long history. Soldiers were dressed in period costumes with hairstyles to match. The military review, I thought, was remarkably ambitious, and apparently it proved to be extraordinarily successful.

On Thursday, October 14, Di and Barry dined with all the other hundreds of invited guests, including Sir Paul Hasluck, Governor-General of Australia, in the great "Club Tent."   Di detailed the menu that evening,

> The food was all specially flown in from Maxim's in Paris, plus the waiters, so it was terribly rich and rare. We started off with caviar and quails' eggs covered with cream, served in a pastry shell, then a mousse of lobster tails, then a saddle of lamb stuffed with truffles . . . followed by a sorbet containing champagne to clear the palate before the main course—Imperial Peacock— which came in on huge silver trays with a cardboard shape covered with peacocks' feathers. . ... The pud was a bit dull . . . a Turban of Figs garnished with raspberries in port.[2]

Long speeches by the shah and Ethiopian Emperor Haile Selassie followed. After a Sound and Light show, they were returned to their hotel, arriving around 4:00 a.m.   What a remarkable, if exhausting, night for them.

On Saturday, I set out for the train station for my return to Mashhad. I thought I had allowed plenty of time, but traffic was even worse than before as all the dignitaries had now arrived back in Tehran. I missed my train and got to spend another day with Ginny.

Time of Discovery

I arrived back in Tehran five days before our wedding. My friends in Mashhad had given me a bachelor party; several of them would be joining us on January 20, as well. There were lots of last-minute details needing attention. We had a meeting with Father O'Farrell and then a rehearsal the day before the wedding. I had to make sure that everything had been arranged for the second reception, which would take place at an Iranian friend's house in the center of the city.

The night before the wedding, my Tuyserkani friends took me to the Moulin Rouge cabaret in Lalezar to celebrate. We partied longer than we should have and did not get to bed until the small

---

[2] Ginny copied Diana Hall's description of events at Persepolis in a letter to her parents, October 19, 1971.

hours of the morning. Then I had to get up early to pick up my suit from the tailor. My friends were still asleep when I left.

The ceremony was scheduled for 2:30 p.m., and I arrived early. Father O'Farrell took one look at me and offered a whiskey. I think he must have thought that I was nervous about the wedding, or maybe he suspected the truth.

Quickly the small church filled with Australian, American, British and Iranian friends and well-wishers. The three Hall boys, home for the long Australian school holidays, served as ushers and Libby as flower girl. The ceremony was relatively brief for there was no sermon. At one point Ginny and I and our four witnesses went into the small room off the sanctuary to sign the marriage register. There was Mr. Avedissian, who had recently pressed Ginny to pay him more money for his services, beaming from ear to ear. At least he had turned up. That formal matter completed, we progressed up the aisle to the waiting limousine—on loan from the Australian ambassador.

Ebrahim, the driver, whisked us north to Tajrish, and we arrived at the residence before any of our guests. It had snowed the night before in the northern part of the city, so traffic was moving more slowly than usual. The light snow was beginning to melt just as we arrived.

Soon, we were in the receiving line welcoming our guests from Tehran and Mashhad. Most were Ginny's friends. I had met many of them but knew only a few well. On my side were my colleagues from Mashhad, and Dr. Dorry, whom I had not seen since my stay in Armish-Maag hospital. Then, to my great surprise, appeared eight of my closest Tuyserkani friends, husbands and wives, the latter having obviously spent the previous day at the beauty salon, while their menfolk cavorted at the Moulin Rouge. The three brothers, Mansur, Teimour, and Nasrollah Ehsani, all with their wives, their brother-in-law, Ghassem Bashiri, and Seyed Mahmud Emami, whose sons I had taught during my time in Tuyserkan, passed through the line. (Due to a mix-up regarding the wedding date, Ehsani, who had been posted to distant Marivan in Kurdistan, had not been able to attend.) They quickly made themselves at home. My worries about their not being comfortable at this first reception were clearly unwarranted. Fortunately, the Halls would be celebrating Australia Day several days later, so the cook had prepared more food than would be needed for the reception, or so he thought. Always masterful in crisis situations, Di gave the order to bring forth part of this reserve.

After picture-taking on the spiral staircase, many toasts, and the cutting of a magnificent wedding cake, baked "informally" by the British Ambassador's chef, we departed for our room at the Hotel Napoleon. After a bit of a break, we set off, still in wedding clothes, for the second reception in the evening. The hosts seated us on a raised platform in the middle of the room while Iranian friends and their extended families mingled and chatted around us. Although we were pretty tired, we enjoyed ourselves and stayed late into the night.

The next day we flew to Isfahan for our brief honeymoon, staying at the Shah Abbas Hotel. This had served as a caravansary during the Safavid dynasty and had been remodeled into a luxury hotel in recent years. The weather in Tehran had turned very cold, but here it was like spring. We did not go touring, but we made a few purchases in the grand, old, covered bazaar. From a small metal-working shop we bought a beautiful, copper candle holder, the craftsmanship of which we still admire.

Back in Tehran, we somehow gathered up Ginny's possessions and our wedding presents, said farewell to the Halls, and set off for the train station. We had a compartment to ourselves all the way to Mashhad, which was totally unexpected. As it turned out ours was the last train into the city for some time. Unusually frigid and snowy weather had swept in around us from the Russian steppes, the so-called "Great Blizzard of 1972." The city was virtually cut off for two weeks.

I had managed to get a message to Osra, our part-time maid, and she had the heaters going and lunch prepared when we arrived. She was a great cook. I had hired her in December when I first moved into our house on Adalat Street. Over the coming days, as familiar meat supplies disappeared from the butcher shops, Osra had to buy what was available, so for a while we ate *khoresh* made with camel instead of lamb or beef. We hardly noticed.

As the temperature continued to drop, our water pipes, which had no insulation, froze, so we ended up going out to the public baths. This was not pleasant. Fortunately, the thaw came after a week of trudging to the baths. We still had to make the obligatory trip through the snow to our outside WC. That winter the snowbanks on either side of the path grew to be taller than Ginny. What a change for her from the residence in Tajrish with its indoor plumbing.

One silver lining to all this snowfall was the early morning melodious call of the *barfi*, advertising his readiness to clear the snow-covered roof. All the traditional adobe houses such as ours required their attention whenever snow was heavy. We became quite familiar with them that winter.

In spite of the bad weather, we had lots of company. We spent many long evenings under the korsi, which I had brought from Tuyserkan, snacking and talking with friends and colleagues. Quite a few of the Peace Corps Volunteers from Group 31, who had trained in Hamadan the previous summer, had been assigned to Khorasan. They came frequently to our house. Neil Smith, whom we both knew and liked very much, came from time to time. He was serving in Kalat-e Naderi, a small town up in the mountains right on the Soviet border. He had to have a special clearance in order to serve in that sensitive area. Although it was not far as the crow flies, it took many hours on poor roads to get there. We tried during the shah's birthday break in October 1972, to visit him, but we could find no buses going there. We never were able to keep our promise to visit him. Others, including Ray Cowart, Hal Aoki, and Sharon and Chris Cockcroft also visited. Then there were visitors from Tehran and abroad and American teachers from Alam and the university and from the British Council, as well. And we were invited out as often as we entertained at home.

All of this, of course, proved a far different lifestyle than the one I had lived in Tuyserkan. Sadly, I established no lasting friendships with any Iranian during my two years in Mashhad. I had feared this might be the case when I was considering whether or not to teach at Alam. Still, it was Iran, and I was enjoying the day-to-day experiences different though they may be.

Although winters could be harsh, and the winter of 1971-1972, was particularly so, warmer weather was never far off. Usually, by early March, winter had disappeared in most parts of the country and that was our experience in Mashhad. We gladly welcomed the Iranian New Year.

We decided to set off for a few days in Afghanistan once the school holidays began. Ruth Stevenson, a middle-aged American teacher at the university, traveled with us to Herat from whence she planned to fly to Kabul. We had initially arranged to spend the entire holiday there, but the university had suddenly announced that those of us on contract could not spend more than five days outside Iran.

The journey from Mashhad to Herat, which should have taken at most eight hours, lasted two days. We crossed into Afghanistan at the Islam Qala entry point without any problem, but then we discovered that the road ahead had been cut in several places by flash flooding, and the water was still too deep to cross. It was getting dark, so I looked for a place to stay. There was little accommodation there at the border and no restaurants. I managed to get us a rather rundown mud hut for the night. It did have a small brazier where we could have a fire. For dinner we ate what was left of the large lunch Ginny had packed the day before. Ruth stayed with the two of us. She wanted to bring in a few of the half-wild dogs that roamed about to keep us warm, but we suggested that was not a good idea.

Ruth was quite an eccentric; one never knew exactly what to expect. She had first come to Iran in the 1950s with her husband. He had suffered an injury shortly after their arrival and had spent the remainder of his life in a wheelchair. After his death, she returned to Iran on something of a mission, to experience the country the way they had intended two decades earlier. Unfortunately, she encountered many discipline problems with her students at the university, and she received little support from her colleagues. In spite of her eccentricities, we found her to be good company, for she was a keen observer of her surroundings.

After an almost sleepless night, we happily boarded a minibus for Herat, hoping the flood had subsided. At the first crossing, the driver had to decide whether or not to ford the swiftly flowing stream, so we all piled out to watch five young Pakistani men confidently drive their Chevrolet sedan into the water, only to have it slowly washed downstream. They clambered to shore. Soon all we could see was a bit of the roof above the muddy water. While we were gazing on this unusual sight, our driver decided to cross—without his passengers. He made a successful crossing, but then we had to go to him on foot. I piggy-backed Ginny, wading through the knee-deep water, hoping I would not lose my footing. Another volunteer brought Ruth over. After a few brusque words to the driver, we took our seats and off we sped.

Soon we arrived at another flooded creek and once again the driver wanted to assess the situation. There was a simple hotel-cum-restaurant here, but we made sure we stayed close to the minibus, so the driver could not abandon us a second time. When it came time to leave, however, Ruth had disappeared. After several anxious minutes, I found her sitting on the floor in a dimly lit room, in a circle of Afghan men, dipping her fingers into a large bowl of rice. She was thoroughly enjoying the company. We finally arrived in Herat late in the afternoon, and Ruth set off for the airport.

We made the most of the time we had left there. We spent many hours with Ahmad Baradaran a local shopkeeper, who was recommended to us by a friend. He turned out to be a charming companion, and we ate most of our midday meals with him right there among the piles of carpets and other textiles. We ended up buying a lovely small tribal carpet and an old qilim with wonderful natural dyes and geometric shapes. We had never seen anything quite like it. Ahmad spoke some English, and the lingua franca of Afghanistan is Dari, a dialect of Persian, so we had no problem communicating.[3]

Herat had some wonderful historical buildings from its heyday as the capital of the Timurid dynasty in the fifteenth century and some from even earlier. We especially enjoyed the Friday Mosque a beautifully tiled complex near the center of the city, which dated from the early 13th century. Another site, Gazar Gah, was a 15th century shrine to the Muslim saint Khoja Abdullah Ansari. When we visited, this building still served as a place of *bast* or sanctuary. Once inside its gateway, criminals or accused could not be taken by the police as long as they did not violate the rules of the shrine. Iran had also once had such traditional places of refuge, but they disappeared in the wave of modernization. At Gazar Gah, we walked among groups of Afghan men who lived on charity from visitors and the shrine authorities.

Our trip back to Mashhad was much less eventful than the outward journey. We enjoyed one day at home before setting off for Tehran. We had intended to go on to Tuyserkan, but when I telephoned, most of my friends had left town for the holiday, so we went south instead. We visited Kashan, a small city on the edge of the desert, famous for the Bagh-e Fin, a superbly designed Persian garden complex dating to the late sixteenth century. I had first visited the city during my training program almost four years earlier.

---

[3] Interestingly, Dari uses many old Persian vocabulary words, which have gone out of common use in Iran, for example "amukhtam" versus "yad gereftam" for "I learned."

The city has an interesting, covered bazaar, and in one of the shops I found an old mirror set in a fine silver frame. I bargained with the shopkeeper, but we could not agree on the price, so I left. A short while later I came to my senses and went back to pay what he had asked. Sadly, the shop was closed. We were leaving on the evening train for Yazd, so I would have to go without the mirror. Hard bargaining did not always succeed.

I had also visited Yazd with Sally in 1970. It was a great desert center with an imposing mosque and city gate. We visited the Zoroastrian fire temple. The white-robed priest tended the eternal flame. Most of Iran's remaining community of believers, about thirty thousand strong, lived in Yazd. Two Zoroastrian Towers of Silence (*Dakhmeh*) lay just outside the city. They had earlier been used for open-air burials, so as not to pollute the earth with corpses, but they were no longer functioning. We visited the site late in the day and as there was no transportation back to town, we had to walk a few miles across the desert. We took care not to tumble into any of the *qanats,* open wells dotting the landscape. Of more immediate concern, however, were the howls we heard all around us. I took off my belt with its large buckle, prepared, if necessary, to defend us against wild dogs or wolves. Fortunately, we arrived back at our hotel unscathed.

Traditional architectural design could be observed everywhere. Of particular interest were the *badgir* or wind towers attached to most houses. These faced the direction of the prevailing hot desert winds, drawing them down two or three stories into the basements of the old homes. The air cooled substantially as it descended, providing a natural air conditioning for the residents in summer.

From Yazd we traveled by bus over the long desert road through Tabas and Ferdows. We stayed overnight with Jerry Glackin, the volunteer in Tabas and strolled in the beautiful city garden, with its overly friendly pelican. Jerry had an attractive old home but no running water. We arrived back in Mashhad just in time for the start of classes at Alam.

There could be little comparison between Tuyserkan and Mashhad. Tuyserkan was an isolated town, with few travelers passing through; Mashhad proved just the opposite. Located on the main land route between South Asia and Europe, a steady stream of foreigners passed through it. We encountered a number of these travelers while living in the city, but our house was far away from the city center, and few strangers ever found their way to our door.

Many Western youths passing through Mashhad showed little sensitivity for the local culture and its taboos and often behaved as if they were at home. I sometimes went down to the shrine area on business and saw young men and women in shorts and cut-off sleeves, sitting with their feet in the empty *joob* calling out loudly to each other, seemingly oblivious to their surroundings. No one in Iran wore shorts in public, and women were expected to cover their arms and hair as well. Men, too, were expected to dress modestly, especially in the vicinity of the shrine. I was surprised that ugly incidents between Mashhadis and young foreigners happened so infrequently.

On special occasions we went to events at the British Council, which was located in a beautiful old compound that had originally housed British consular officials. The extensive gardens surrounding the buildings had been laid out with great artistry. This complex was a legacy of the Great Game with the Russians at the end of the 19th century, when the two Great Powers had vied with each other for dominance in the region.

The council provided English classes and sponsored various cultural events. Our friends, Rosalind Wilson and Paul Attar, taught there. During our time, the head of the organization was a well-meaning but quite inept middle-aged British man with a young wife and two small children. Ginny became good friends with her. Sadly, her husband had a drinking problem and sometimes turned up at these affairs mildly inebriated. This was taboo as far as Iranians were concerned.

We also came to know Mary Harvey, who had arrived in Mashhad in the 1920s as a young nurse to work at the Presbyterian hospital. As in Hamadan, the Mashhad hospital had been sold to the government. Mary stayed on to train young Iranian women as nurses. She had many colorful stories to tell about her early years in the city.

Our first excursion as newlyweds outside Mashhad had almost ended in disaster. Carter and Judy had asked us to join them for a picnic at Akhlamad about sixty kilometers west of the city. We would be chaperoning a bus full of Iranian students from the IAS. After we arrived, Ginny suggested the two of us climb up a steep slope to get a better view. It was a talus slope composed of broken pieces of rock from the cliffs above. We climbed higher and higher until Ginny suddenly cried out that she could not move in any direction for fear of slipping. I managed to get myself over to the side of the steep slope. Then, I worked my way back toward her, gradually coaxing her to reach out to take my hand. She did, and we moved slowly toward safety. All this time, we had many concerned on-lookers below. After this drama, we decompressed by visiting the waterfalls for which the site is well known. It attracted many visitors, including skilled rock climbers, from Mashhad.

A number of times we visited Brian Street in Zoshk, not far from Akhlamad. It was an apple-growing village in a beautiful valley, with a rushing stream draining the surrounding mountains. At harvest time as you walked out of the village up the broad, slowly rising pathway through the orchards, with their lovely stone walls, you had to share the way with donkeys laden with ripe fruit moving down to the storehouse. With the leaves changing color and the early snows beginning to accumulate on the mountain tops, the whole scene was stunningly beautiful. This was all made possible by an ingenious old, engineering scheme, drawing off a portion of the stream's natural flow high up the valley and carrying it through painfully constructed channels to the orchards. Looking upward from within this man-made paradise, all one saw were the barren hillsides of the towering mountains.

Barry Hall came to visit on some official duty, and he remained an extra day to make the journey out to Zoshk with us. We pulled up in the rutted lane in the ambassador's limousine with Ebrahim at the wheel. What a sight for everyone in the village; the children clustered around this never-before-seen vehicle. Brian was still in residence, and we had a wonderful day together. I can still see Brian and Barry, both of whom had slight hearing impairments, walking along in front of us with their heads tilted toward each other obviously engrossed in their conversation. Barry always seemed happiest when he was out in the countryside away from all the formalities of the capital.

Brian had not been able to obtain a long-term residence permit, so he had to leave the country every three months. He had used the Afghan border at Islam Qala too many times, so in the late spring he decided to travel all the way south to Zahedan, a twenty-four-hour bus trip. There, he crossed and re-crossed the Iran-Pakistan border. When he returned, Andre Singer and he were setting out by jeep for northern Afghanistan where Andre had research to carry out.

I also had to renew my residence permit regularly, but I only had to travel downtown to the police station. I always felt rather uncomfortable when I did this, for inevitably there would be a large group of Afghan men sitting around the walls waiting to have their business attended to. They had probably been waiting for hours. In I walked, and the sergeant on duty would motion me over to the desk. He looked at my papers and took my permit to be stamped. I left having spent no more than thirty minutes in the office. What were the Afghans thinking, I wondered, when they saw me being treated in such an efficient manner? Whatever it was, I never noticed any change in their expressions.

I knew there was not a lot of love lost between Iranian officials and Afghans. The Iranians considered them uncouth and backward; Afghans thought Iranians effete and too full of pride. Herat province had belonged to Iran for centuries until the British snipped it off after the brief Anglo-Persian War in 1857. Since that time, the neighboring regions of Khorasan and Herat had grown to be quite dissimilar, the former brimming with modernity, the latter remaining much as it had always been.

Once the school year ended, we made plans to take home leave in the States during July. Our friend, Tom Gordon, would stay in our house while we were away. Ginny had not met any of my family, nor I hers. We planned to visit the United States in 1972, stopping off in London on the way back to see Ginny's sister, Sheena. The following year, we would settle for a while in Australia, where I would meet my in-laws and Ginny's other relatives and friends for the first time.

What were we thinking as we took off for America? Ginny must have been nervous about meeting all those strangers for the first time, but she never showed any concern. I am afraid I was thinking only about how happy I would be to have them all meet my wonderful wife at last.

We had a good trip bouncing around the country on a special ticket that allowed us to make many flights in a short period of time: Boston, Hyannis, Pensacola, New Orleans, Washington, New York, Springfield, Boston. We enjoyed our brief stays with family and friends in all these places. Ginny and my sister, Ann, established an especially close and lasting bond. In New York City, we met the Travelsteads with whom I had worked the previous summer in Hamadan. Then, we had a reunion with Sally Chaffee, whom I had last seen as she pulled out of the Tehran bus depot the previous June headed for Europe. We had already reconnected with John Giordano who was back in Iran heading his second TEFL training program for the Peace Corps.

It was election year in America, and together we watched some of the Democratic political convention, where George McGovern won the nomination. Ginny found the process somewhat bizarre. She could not quite understand why the delegates went on with all their shenanigans and flowery speeches. This public spectacle was unlike anything she had ever seen.

Next, a flight to London for a warm meeting with my sister-in-law. Ginny and Sheena had not seen each other in over three years, so they had a lot to catch up on. We invited Sheena to visit us in Mashhad, but she was not able to make the trip before we left the following year.

Landing in Tehran, we had planned to take the train to Mashhad immediately, but we were delayed. An important benefactor, who had given money and land to the Shrine of the Eighth Imam in Mashhad, had passed away, and all the flights and trains to Mashhad were sold out as throngs of mourners headed there for the funeral. After the unexpected delay, our arrival home was all the sweeter. As I arrived two days later than expected, however, the university took away our housing allowance for the time we were abroad and docked my pay two hundred dollars, even though my summer classes did not begin until the day after we reached Mashhad. What an unpleasant welcome that was.

Osra, our maid, had taken advantage of our being away, letting the house get rather messy. Added to this, she had taken a holiday for herself for part of the month in spite of the fact that we had arranged time off for her when we got back. The problem was, Osra loved to cook, but she was never fond of doing housework. It would remain a continuing challenge to get her to do some of both.

After summer classes had finished, the university agreed that we could travel within Iran before the start of the school year at the end of September. We went straight to the bazaar to buy turquoise for two friends in Tehran with whom we often stayed. Ben was Austrian and Rosemary, Australian. Ben told us that in Europe people prized turquoise that had dark streaks and other blemishes in it. Iranians preferred the pure blue stones, so what Ben wanted was relatively inexpensive and easy to obtain.

We visited our friend, Mehdi Djavedani, who specialized in turquoise for which the Mashhad area was famous. We often visited his shop even when we did not intend to buy anything. Sometimes we brought friends to buy souvenirs of their visit. Once, I had him make a nice bracelet of green agates set in gold, which I gave to

Ginny the Christmas before we married. A few days later we were at a party at the University Club, and the bracelet slipped off her wrist and into the WC—No retrieving that! She was desolate, so we went back to the shop and bought a large green turquoise pendant, set in worked gold. The stone may have come originally from the Negev desert.

After we had made our purchases at Mehdi's shop, we set off for Tehran, spending the night with Ben and Rosemary. We gave them the turquoise as a parting gift. They planned to leave Iran before our return.

Then we traveled on to Tuyserkan and a great reunion. We stayed again at the Hotel Alvand and our friends invited us to their homes for most meals. Mansur and his young wife now had an infant daughter. In one notable cross-cultural moment, Azam teased Mansur, saying he should give her the attention that I gave Ginny. In another, a group of women took Ginny aside and peppered her with intimate questions about our sex life. She pretended not to understand.

Mansur Dabaghi invited us to dinner in his garden above the town. Oh, what memories that brought back. We thoroughly enjoyed our several days together there, realizing that each return might be our last.

No sooner had we arrived back in Mashhad than guests began to turn up. John Giordano en route to Afghanistan, came to stay. Then we invited Neil Smith, who was staying alone in a hotel, to stay with us. He did not get into Mashhad often from his post in Kalat-e Naderi, and we enjoyed his company. Other Peace Corps Volunteers came as well, some to a meal, others to stay a night or two. They were making the most of the last days of summer before the schools opened again. We managed to accommodate many of them, even though our house was quite small.

That fall, Ginny started doing office work five mornings a week at the university's English Literature Faculty. She worked for eight faculty, a mix of Americans and Iranians, men and women. They kept her terribly busy, but they were a very congenial group. One of them Edie Zareen, an American, became a close friend of Ginny's. She had married Mohammad (Moie) Zareen in California and recently returned to Iran. She knew remarkably little about the country before she arrived.

We often went with guests and friends such as the Zareens to one of our favorite restaurants in Mashhad, Kareem Shisliki, which was on the outskirts of town. It served wonderful meat dishes. It sold alcohol as well, and we had some uproarious times there. Sometime after we left the city, the owner went on pilgrimage to Mecca, and when he came back, he stopped serving liquor. The meat, I was told by friends, just did not taste the same after that.

In the heart of the city, a lunch-time favorite was the Iran Hotel. The restaurant served a variety of excellent *khoreshes*, which were usually found only in Iranian homes. Most restaurants specialized in grilled meat dishes, so this was a treasure.

For a long time, I had wanted to improve my reading and writing of Persian. I finally had the chance when I arranged with Ali Vusughi to teach me at home two days a week. He was an excellent teacher, who had worked in several Peace Corps training programs. The trainees thought he was wonderful. Under his tutelage, my language skills began to improve, but it was a slow process.

One day when he came, I told him I had just finished reading E. G. Browne's history of the early twentieth century Iranian Constitutional Revolution. Browne wrote a lot about groups of Iranian dissidents who had worked clandestinely to promote the political reforms of the day. I asked Ali where such people could be found in the 1970s. I thought he would shrug his shoulders, but instead he replied that there were many such individuals right in Mashhad, but that being a foreigner it was unlikely I would know anything about them. Later, when the revolution came, and Mashhad became an important center of unrest, I recalled his words.

In those years there were very few signs—at least to us—of what the future might hold for Iran. Diana Hall had written that the day after our wedding, she and Barry were escorted home from the palace by an armed guard, following a bomb-throwing incident near the American embassy. Then, we read that a terrorist group had attacked a gendarmerie post in the mountains north of Tehran. University students, of course, were always ready to go on strike, but they seemed to focus on local issues. Brian Street, who supported them, had a scary experience one night after having dinner with us. A stranger hopped into the taxi next to him and made a sign as if slashing his throat. Then, he quickly disappeared. Brian presumed he was a member of the secret police (SAVAK), who must have been following him. Once when we hailed a taxi, we saw a young man in clerical garb seated alone in the backseat. The driver asked him to move to the front so we could get in. This was common practice. The man, refusing to ride with a woman without hijab, jumped out, hurled the fare at the driver, and stomped off down the road. The driver cursed him loudly. We did not quite know what to make of this situation, which we had never experienced before. Yet, the sum of these isolated events did not augur revolutionary change.

We had a surprise visit in October from the elder Mr. and Mrs. Ehsani and two friends. They had come on pilgrimage to the shrine. They came on a day when Osra was cooking up a storm in the kitchen, so we had soup, roast chicken, celery khoresh, mounds of rice with saffron and a massive plate of fresh fruit. What a delight to be able to entertain them in our home after all the hospitality they had extended to me during my years in Tuyserkan.

During the few days' break from classes for the celebration of the shah's birthday on October 26, we decided to go to Nishapur, just ninety minutes away. The Mongols had sacked this ancient city in the early 13th century. It never recovered its former glory. We had the ancient ruins all to ourselves. At the hotel we heard that an Australian had been arrested for killing a young Iranian bicyclist with his car. We could hear the sounds of the prison inmates coming in our window from the jail next door. We decided to try to pay him a visit but thought we would encounter a lot of red tape. Surprisingly, they let us in to see him almost immediately.

It turned out that Jordan was originally from Bulgaria but had spent several years working on the railroads in Australia. He was not an Australian citizen, but when he wanted to return to Europe to see his parents, he had obtained a laissez-passer travel document from Canberra. He had to return to Australia by a set date, or he might not be able to return at all.

He had planned to go to Yugoslavia, where he would have a reunion with his family. Then he would go on to Germany to buy a used Mercedes Benz, which he would drive to Afghanistan and sell at a profit. Then he would get work on a merchant ship traveling from Sri Lanka to Australia.

When he arrived in Belgrade, he discovered that border controls had been tightened, and his family could not leave Bulgaria. In great sadness, he set out to accomplish the rest of his plan. Having bought the car, he departed for Afghanistan, getting as far as Nishapur, where he accidently killed the young bicyclist. He confided to me that he knew beforehand the car brakes needed work.

So, there he was sitting in his cell waiting for a trial date. Fortunately for him, the family of the boy had agreed to accept so-called "blood money," that is the payment of a sum determined by them, which would allow him to go free after a trial. He had paid the money, so he would serve no sentence.

He remained in prison throughout the early winter months awaiting trial. He was moved to Mashhad, but I was not allowed to visit him there, although I sent him notes from time to time. Finally, in late December, he received a date for his trial. I attended the session and to me it seemed well organized and fair. The judgment of the court was that he should be set free, but he could never drive again in Iran.

Then, he became trapped in a catch-22 situation. The police did not release him, claiming that his three-month visa had expired. They shipped him to Tehran and from there to the Turkish border, where border guards would not allow him to leave, without the vehicle that had been noted in his travel document when he first arrived. Finally, they relented, and he went first to Ankara and then on to Istanbul. Eventually, he received an Iranian visa and returned to reclaim his car, which he believed the chief of police in Nishapur had confiscated for himself.

When he turned up at our house, I warned him about driving in Iran again, but he paid me little heed. I thought he had a lot of determination but not much sense. He took a long shower and stayed the night. He explained he had taken so much time in the shower because he wanted to make sure he did not have any lice. Amazingly, the next day he returned with his car. After lunch, he set out for the Afghan border. I gave him some money as he was by then almost penniless.

That was the last we heard of him until five years later. By an amazing coincidence, the teacher who was hired to replace me at the Convent of the Sacred Heart School in Sydney in 1978, was married to a Bulgarian woman. She knew that Jordan had returned safely to Australia and that he was working in the opal mines in Coober Pedy in the Outback. We were pleased to learn that the tale had a happy ending.

In late November Osra gave us notice that she would be leaving in a fortnight. I had dismissed her earlier, but when she burst into tears, I had relented. Our relationship had been strained ever since her dereliction of duty in the summer. She had worked for a number of Americans previously, and I think she had pretty much been her own boss, doing what she liked. She was not happy that Ginny was always asking her to do housework, especially once Ginny started working at the university.

We thought that she was single when she came to us, but then she announced one day that she was married and pregnant. Apparently, she had contracted a temporary marriage *(sighe),* which was allowed under Twelver Shia law. This was a device which served pilgrims and traders, who traveled far from home for long periods of time. A man might reside for a long period in Mashhad, for example, and while he was there, he and his temporary spouse could live together as husband and wife. A contract specified the length of marriage, the sum to be paid to the bride and arrangements for any children born to this short-term union. Sunni Muslims scorned the practice as did many Iranians, but it continued in Mashhad and elsewhere in Iran.

Ginny was relieved that the tense situation had finally resolved itself, and we could look for someone to replace Osra. Ginny's culinary skills had grown exponentially over the previous year, so we did not need a cook any longer. We wanted someone who could keep the house clean and tidy while we both worked.

We found that someone, in Fatimeh—who had never worked for foreigners. She had come to Mashhad from her village and lived with her married daughter. She was an awfully hard worker and very responsible. She seemed to know just what needed to be done. Unlike her predecessor, she had a sweet disposition, and she was completely trustworthy. Happily, she worked for us until we left Mashhad.

That winter of 1973 brought an unexpected tragedy to our small group of friends. It concerned Edie and Moie Zareen. Ginny and Edie had become close friends at the university, and they spent a lot of time together. We socialized quite a bit with both of them as well.

Theirs was not an enviable situation. Moie, an only son, had spent many years in California, where he met and married Edie. While a student there, he had led protests against the shah, which were increasing abroad during the late 1960s and early 1970s. No doubt agents of SAVAK, the secret police organization, had taken note. Then his father became extremely ill and under much pressure as an only son, Moie decided he had to return to Mashhad. Edie came also, and they lived with his parents and his unmarried sister.

Moie had taught elementary school before he went to America, and he had been quite successful. When he returned, however, he could not find work. It seemed that the regime stood in his way. Thus, their only income was what Edie earned at the university teaching English. She was such a gentle and innocent soul, all of this must have come as a great shock to her, but she remained cheerful.

One February day, Edie arrived at the university full of excitement. She told Ginny that she and Moie were going to Tehran, just the two of them, for a wonderful "weekend" away. She had bought a new dress and was heading to the hairdresser that afternoon. That was the last time Ginny saw her.

A few days later it was reported that the couple had been found dead in their Tehran hotel room. There was a garbled story about accidental poisoning from a bottle of wine. Other rumors circulated that they had committed suicide because of Moie's desperate situation. Many whispered that SAVAK might have had a part in their deaths. We never knew what had really happened, but we were immensely saddened by the loss of our two friends.

Later, when we were in Tehran, we visited the US Consul at the embassy. He asked us a lot of questions about Edie and Moie, but he did not provide any new information. If he knew more about their deaths, he did not share it with us.

In spite of our sorrow, life moved on. February was the slow season for tourists in Herat, and our friend, Ahmad, decided to set off for Baghdad with two teacher friends to purchase merchandise for his shop. They turned up unannounced at our door one afternoon when I was at work. When Ginny opened the door, Ahmad's friends, who had never traveled outside Afghanistan, got quite a surprise seeing her without hijab. Anyway, they would not come in because I was not present.

When Ginny told me later what had happened, I immediately recalled an experience in Tuyserkan, when I had broken this taboo, not once but several times. I would drop by my good friend Hashem's house to see him, and if he were not at home, his wife would invite me to come in and wait until he returned. She was practicing *taarof,* an important and elaborate system of Iranian courtesy, and I should have said that I would come back later; instead, I went in. Only much later did I learn that my behavior had caused a good deal of gossip, and, of course, I was fully to blame. Hashem never said a word about my lapses.

Anyway, Ahmad came alone to lunch with us the next day. He brought some carpets that he wanted to sell, so we invited a few friends to come to our house to have a look. He sold several of them. He soon set out with his companions, promising to stop in on his return from Iraq.

Ginny certainly had a number of adjustments to make, living in Mashhad. She had given up a lot of the independence she had enjoyed so much in Tehran. There were many fewer English speakers in Mashhad, and her Persian had not developed as she first hoped. Therefore, we often attended to business matters together, so that I could translate. And now that she was married, the banks and other agencies wanted to be assured that her husband approved of any business transactions. Furthermore, she could not wander easily on her own downtown.

I, too, had had to adapt, becoming much more of a protector when we were out in public, whereas previously I had only been concerned about myself. I remember one incident in Tehran that brought this all home to me in an instant. We were walking together in Tajrish circle before our wedding. Ginny was dressed modestly but not in hijab. We passed a group of teenage boys who made some sexist comments that made me bristle. When one of them brushed his hand against her as we passed, I grabbed him, gave him a tongue-lashing in my best colloquial Persian, and added a kick in the seat of his pants for good measure. I am sure this hurt me more than it did him. Had I become, I wondered, the Ugly American?

Travel always relieved our daily stresses, and, as the No Ruz holiday approached, we began to make plans for what would be our last extended trip. The university, that fickle institution, had decided to allow us to go abroad, so we chose to spend our time exploring Afghanistan beyond Herat. As usual we dreamed of going further than either time or money would allow.

I had to take care of a number of bureaucratic details before we could leave. I obtained a permission letter from the university, then a clearance from the police, and finally another one from the tax office. After that, I could apply for Afghan visas. I hoped it would all be worth the effort.

On the first day, it took twelve hours to travel from Mashhad to Herat. The problem was always the two border posts; the road distance was only 380 kilometers (228 miles). Once we arrived, we spent much of the day with Ahmad and walking around the city. His mother had prepared a wonderful dinner for us, which we ate with him and his brothers in the shop. We never met any of the women in his family.

Next day we set off for Qandahar, which had a reputation for being unfriendly toward foreigners. The previous year, several hippies, high on hashish, had been hacked to death in a hostel there by a group of religious zealots. The perpetrators were hanged in public. We wandered around the bazaar and made a few purchases, and no one troubled us. We had to stay two nights in the city because we could not get bus tickets to go on immediately to Kabul.

In the capital we stayed only a short time before catching a small prop plane to Bamiyan Valley in the center of the country. In mid-March, the only way to reach the isolated valley was by air, for the passes were still blocked with snow. The pilot could not fly over the high mountains, so he flew through them, which made for some exciting moments. I turned slightly green as the tiny plane bobbed and weaved its way to our destination.

On our flight, there was a Peace Corps Afghanistan couple, who had been in Bamiyan only a short time. We also talked with another passenger, a German Volunteer worker, who had already spent a year in the valley. We tended to forget that several European countries had their own Volunteer services. Anyway, the three of them gave us a lot of useful information.

They forgot, however, one particularly important fact. We intended to stay at the government guest house for tourists, which other travelers had recommended. Unfortunately, we quickly discovered that the lodge had not yet opened for the season. We learned this just as the plane was taxiing down the runway and about to disappear into the Hindu Kush, not to return for four days.

The volunteers recommended a nearby teahouse as the only option for accommodation. This was the most basic setting imaginable. Our room had no heat or running water; we washed in a bucket of cold water. The bedding was damp; it tended finally to dry out from our body warmth just as it was time to get up each morning. We were the sole guests.

The only warm room was the tea house itself, which was the domain of men. We did not see another woman in our entire time in Bamiyan. The proprietor allowed Ginny to come into the room if she sat near the door, looking as if she were about to depart. We ate simple fare, bread, boiled eggs, and tea. We survived, although Ginny came back with a raging cold.

All those difficulties aside, the valley itself was glorious. The Hazara who lived here were largely Shia Muslims, a minority in the country. Along one towering wall we could see quite close to us the famous statues of Buddha carved out of the rocky hillside in the 6th Century CE, when the valley was a thriving Buddhist center, before the rise of Islam. The height of the taller one stood at 53 meters (174 feet) and the smaller one at 35 meters (115 feet). Around and behind the statues was a maze of passageways and caves. We climbed a hidden staircase to stand on the head of the larger statue. Originally, everything had been covered in Buddhist iconography, but most of that work had disappeared or faded over the centuries. Still, the views were stunning. Looking out from the top of the head, we could see the whole valley spread out below.[4]

The countryside was just beginning to show signs of spring. The river through the valley was rushing with runoff from the snow-capped peaks, and some green foliage had appeared. We spent hours walking around the valley on our own. One day we hired a driver to take us to the mouth of the valley, which opened into the side of a dramatic U-shaped valley with sheer walls carved by glacial action. We hiked to the top of the entrance, where we found a few old guard posts in what was called the Red City, due to the color of the building material. Only this remained after the Mongols sacked the city and the valley beyond in the thirteenth century.

When the plane returned, we were waiting on the runway. For some reason, the German Volunteer was returning with us. That night he led us to an excellent Italian restaurant run by an expatriate. Next morning, we set off for Jalalabad several hours down the road toward the border with Pakistan and the city of Peshawar. It was much warmer at the lower elevation. There was a considerable Indian influence, and many of the shops were owned by Sikhs. The next day we went out to Hadda another ancient Buddhist center that had been largely excavated by the French in the 1920s.

We returned briefly to Kabul and then retraced our route to Herat. Ahmad insisted on taking us out to lunch at a well-known *kebabi*. As we entered the door-less restaurant, we passed sheep carcasses, hanging from hooks at the door. Once seated at a small table, we could not help being distracted by the mice skittering over our feet as we tried to tell Ahmad about our trip. The kebabs were exceptionally good. Once again, Ginny was the only woman in sight. Western women often become "honorary men" in such an environment, and they can go where no Afghan woman would venture even in their all-enveloping *chadris*. Only in Kabul had we

---

[4] The Taliban destroyed the Buddhas in 2001.

seen women on the streets and only a minority of those were in Western dress.

We wanted to buy a larger sized Baluchi carpet, so I asked Ahmad if he would help me find a good quality one. He agreed, but it soon became apparent that he felt awkward going to his friends' shops with me. If he gave me the advice I wanted, he risked offending them. Finally, he asked me to leave a sum of money with him; he would pick out a fine carpet for us and send it to Mashhad. That sounded like an excellent idea. I also agreed to make him a short-term loan as he was temporarily low on cash and needed to make some purchases for his shop.

The trip back to Mashhad proved uneventful. We even had a few days to rest up before starting work again. It had been an exhausting, but wonderful, holiday. Fatimeh had the place spic and span when we arrived home, even though she, too, had traveled during No Ruz, going on pilgrimage all the way to Qom.

A few weeks later an Afghan appeared at our door, carrying a large parcel. Ahmad had sent it, he said. We thanked him and took it inside. We opened it quickly to find the most beautiful Baluchi carpet we had ever seen. Two and a half meters long and one and a half meters wide and covered with geometric designs in red and black, it still gets much attention and many compliments from our guests. Ahmad had done us a great service.

Then, in late August, two weeks before we left Mashhad, Bill Hanaway, a Persian scholar from the University of Pennsylvania, whom we did not know, knocked on our door. He had just arrived from Herat with a package from Ahmad. Inside was the two hundred dollars I had loaned my friend five months earlier. That would come in handy on our upcoming travels.

One final dramatic and unexpected change in our lives took place that last spring. We were sleeping in our guest room because we had turned over our bedroom to a visiting Australian friend. During the night we kept hearing tiny noises, which we assumed were mice scurrying around in the walls. Next morning, I went off early to teach. When I returned, Ginny had quite a story to tell. When she had come home from work, Fatimeh came running out to meet her. She was terribly upset. Ginny quickly discovered that the noises of the previous night had come from kittens hidden away inside my desk. The mother cat must have crept in through the open window the day before and had her litter in my open-backed desk to keep them safe from the tomcat. The mother had returned to take one of the three kittens away, but she had disappeared thereafter. Ginny, thinking that the mother would come back, put the two remaining kittens out in the patio. The tomcat got there first and, to Ginny's horror, killed one. Ginny rescued the other kitten. We had no choice but to keep her.

Josie, we called her, was so young her eyes were barely open, and they were still blue. We doubted that she had even had one drink from her mother. Ginny knew exactly what to do. She fed Josie with an eye dropper, cuddled her on her lap, and at night she wrapped a clock in a towel and placed it next to Josie in her box to simulate her mother's beating heart. With such care and attention, she thrived, and we came to love her dearly.

Fatimeh, of course, had a quite different response. She was at first terrified of the kitten. Iranians do not generally have dogs or cats as pets, and they experience little of that special bond that many Westerners cherish. We had to make sure that they stayed apart. Occasionally, we failed. Then, our maid would run down the hallway, with our wee kitten giving chase. We could not help laughing in spite of ourselves. When we went out, we had to shut Josie in our bedroom. Interestingly, Fatimeh soon got used to the kitten, and within a month or so, she had stopped panicking when Josie appeared. She could even laugh—at a distance— at the kitten's antics in the garden. That was the most we could expect.

Sadly, we knew that when we left Iran in several months, we would not be able to take Josie with us. To bring her into Australia, she would first have to spend six months in quarantine in Britain, then a five-week sea voyage followed by another six months in quarantine in Sydney. To subject her to all that would be cruel, we thought. Therefore, we started searching for a good home; and we found one with a newly arrived Peace Corps couple. In the meantime, she became the focus of our attention.

In June we had to go into Tehran so that I could complete paperwork for entry into Australia at the end of the year. Many of our friends had left the city or were on the point of departing. The Halls had left the previous year for Greece. We spent a few evenings with John Giordano, who had returned for his third and final Peace Corps training program.

In Mashhad after our return, I suddenly became terribly ill, with vomiting and high fever. I quickly became dehydrated. Ginny called our good friends, Zina and Alex Khachatourian, asking for help. She was British and he an Armenian-Iranian cinema owner.

They immediately arranged to take me to a nearby private hospital. It seems I might have had food poisoning from a meal we had at a local restaurant. The doctor prescribed a number of medications. In Iran, hospitals expected family to go to local pharmacies to fill prescriptions and then bring the medications back to be administered by the physician. This is what Ginny had to do. In this case, however, the instructions were in French, so I had to translate them first into Persian. Then, I was put on a drip. The practice of having nurses was in its infancy. The expectation was that family members, a wife or mother, would stay with the patient and look after him. So, Ginny spent the night in the room, watching my drip and hoping for a speedy recovery. Her prayers were answered, and early next morning I was well enough to go home.

Farewell

Shortly after that episode, we hosted a big party for our friends before we packed up our house. We did all the food preparation for thirty people ourselves with Fatimeh's help. I remember sitting on upturned buckets in the tiled shower room, as we cut up a mountain of fruit for what would become gallons of fruit salad. What could we have been thinking? We decorated the courtyard with lights and candles, we put out small tables and cushions for seating and hired two Iranian musicians to play for the evening. It turned out to be quite a success, although the hosts were done in.

We had determined some time earlier that we would leave Iran permanently once my annual contract with the university had ended. We thought that would be in early September. Although we both loved the country and the people, we knew that we would always be foreigners, no matter how long we remained. We had known expatriates who had stayed too long and found the eventual separation traumatic. We hoped to avoid that.

We thus had many preparations to make. I sent countless letters to schools in Australia seeking employment for the school year that would begin in late January. We wanted to sell many of our household items before we left, so there was a constant stream of interested buyers coming through the house. Also, we had to arrange to have much of our clothing and other items shipped, first to Tehran and from there to Sydney.

I went to the bazaar to hire a carpenter to build us a large wooden box for our household items. He did what I asked and had it delivered to our door. It was immense, two meters square. I immediately realized that if we filled it, no one would be able to move it. He had to take it back and turn it into two boxes. That worked much better. Even, then, when the shipment arrived in Sydney and Ginny went down to customs to claim it, she watched in horror as one of the boxes dangled from a crane over the water with the up-side of the box completely open. One wrong move and everything would have sunk to the bottom of Sydney Harbor!

We enjoyed one last visit from Tuyserkani friends before we left. The Bashiris, mother, father, mother-in-law and two children, had come on pilgrimage to the shrine. They spent a week in Mash-had, and we welcomed them to a number of meals. One afternoon they came to our house, and Ginny had just baked a delicious cake, which she offered to everyone. Ghassem's mother politely de-clined, so Ginny went on to serve everyone else. Soon, Ghassem started chuckling, saying his mother had been exercising *taarof.* Ginny was supposed to ask her three times, and the third time it would be polite for his mother to say yes. This misunderstanding cleared up, Ginny gave her a large slice of the much-admired cake.

One day we took them on a picnic to Zoshk, which everyone enjoyed. It remained one of our favorite spots outside the city. We were sad to say good-by to them. I always enjoyed reconnecting with Iranian friends from my Peace Corps days.

Then, the university surprised me one last time by moving up my final workday by two weeks. This meant we would be able to speed up our departure. Knowing this earlier would have been help-ful, I thought.

We were farewelled by many over the last days. The whole process of departing was exhilarating and exhausting. When the time came to leave, we were relieved to slump into our seats on the 5:00 p.m. train to Tehran, as our two-year sojourn in Mashhad came to an end.

How fortunate we had been to spend our early married life to-gether in Mashhad. Although we did not benefit from having fami-ly close by, neither did we have to comply with any of the usual post-nuptial expectations. We were able to get to know each other at our own pace, without external pressure, and in an environment that we both loved so much. Those years provided vivid memories that we have shared for a lifetime.

Our final days in Iran seemed to go by in a rush. In Tehran I arranged for shipping our goods to Sydney. Then we set out for the west of the country to say good-by to old friends. In Hamadan we had dinner with the Birds. No longer a missionary, Jack now worked for the carpet company. Then on to Kermanshah and Ghasr-e Shirin to spend a few days with the Bashiris. From there we made the long bus trip to Marivan located near the mountainous Iraqi border. This small town in Kurdistan was where Mr. Ehsani had been appointed Director of Education in fall 1971.

The Kurds wore their own style of dress accentuated by turbans with fringes. Taller than the average Iranian, they always seemed to me a proud people. The Kurdish population extended over the border into Iraq and Turkey and even as far as northeastern Syria. They had waged intermittent warfare with the several governments where they resided but had never succeeded in creating a permanent nation state of their own.

We stayed with Mr. Ehsani and his family for several days. We enjoyed reminiscing about the times we had spent together in Tuyserkan. We toured the area. There was a small, natural, fresh-water lake on the edge of town. This was quite unusual in Iran, where most lakes on the plateau were located behind man-made dams.

One day we had an exciting excursion to the border village of Baiveh. Ehsani was driving the ministry jeep toward the Iraqi border along a narrow, unpaved road with the two of us and his two sons. Suddenly, two Kurdish irregulars, brandishing automatic rifles with bandoliers of bullets crisscrossing their chests, leaped into the middle of the road. They looked as if they had stepped out of a Hollywood action film. They pointed their weapons at our driver, demanding to see his papers. Here he was, one of the top government officials in the district having to answer to Iraqi Kurdish guests. He complied, and they let us pass. These warriors were part of the Iraqi-Kurdish forces that the shah had allowed to enter Iranian territory. They controlled a strip of land along the border in this area. They were at war with the Baghdad government, also an enemy of the shah—at least for the present. Eighteen months later the shah would abandon the Iraqi Kurds and seal the border after he made a peace agreement with Saddam Hussein.

We proceeded to the border where the tiny shops, many owned by Iraqi-Kurds, sold goods smuggled from Iraq. While walking in the village, we ran into Andre Singer, one of our anthropologist friends from Mashhad. He was now working for the Granada Television series, "The Disappearing World." He had already worked on an episode in the Pamirs of Afghanistan, and now he was assisting with "The Dervishes of Kurdistan." It was a happy and unexpected reunion. (We saw a preview of the film at Granada studios in London later in the year.)

The next day Ehsani and Mahvash had been invited to a Kurdish village wedding, and they took us along. These were Iranian Kurds. The men gathered on one rooftop, the women on another, while down below men were line dancing in honor of the bride and groom. Later, dinner was served to us all. By tradition, the men ate first.

Next day we took our leave of the Ehsanis and headed to Tuyserkan. It was a familiar road, but this visit, I knew, would be my last. We stayed at the Hotel Alvand and visited several families in town and in the gardens. Each time I had come back, I felt slightly less connected to the town; it pulled less at my heartstrings when I left. This, I supposed, was a good sign.

Back in Tehran we made final arrangements for the trip through Azerbaijan to the Turkish border. We would travel by bus, train and ship to London; we could not resist the lure of an overland journey. We spent a night in Tabriz and visited a few of the sights. Ginny had never been there before. Then we took a bus to Maku, the last Iranian town before the border. I bought a two-volume set of a Persian dictionary in a bookstore there; I had not thought of doing that earlier.

I felt the pressure building the closer we came to the border and the end of my five-and-a-quarter-year sojourn in Iran. I had matured so much in that time, learned so much, now I was about to leave behind a land and people to which I had become intimately attached. The time in Mashhad had helped to loosen the bond a little because I did not live as closely to Iranians as I had in Tuyserkan, nevertheless this moment jolted me. Parting was painful. I was absorbed in my own struggle. For Ginny, the most difficult time had come two weeks earlier when we left our home in Mashhad, Fatimeh, Josie, and our friends. Now, she was looking forward to reunion with her parents, friends and family.

Ginny in Isfahan, Iran, during Indiaman trip, spring 1967

Jim and Ginny with Dr. Dorry, wedding reception, January 20, 1972.

Jim and Tuyserkan friends at wedding. (l. to r.) Seyed Mahmud Emami, Nasrollah Ehsani, Author, Teimour Ehsani, Ghassem Bashiri, and Mansur Ehsani, January 20, 1972.

Barry Hall (Australian Ambassador) offering a toast to bride and groom. Diana Hall in background, January 20, 1972.

Flash flood on road to Herat, March 1972

Baradaran brothers, (l. to r.) Dawood and Ahmad,
Herat, 1972

British Council library and residence, Mashhad, 1972

Ginny and Jim in Zoshk, 1972

Young boy on donkey returning to village with load of
apples, Zoshk, 1972

With Fatimeh in our courtyard,
Mashhad, 1973

Ginny feeding Josie with a
bottle, spring 1973

Giant Buddha at Bamiyan, Afghanistan, March 1973

Proud owner at entrance to his kebabi,
Herat, March 1973

Mr. Ehsani, Saeed, Masoud and Mahtab (l. to r.) at lunch, Marivan,
September 1973

3

Iran from Afar (Mostly), 1973-2017

Down Under at Last

We crossed into Turkey on September 21, 1973. The only bright moment in that otherwise sad day was a glorious view to the north of snow-capped Mount Ararat (elevation 5,137 m.) Although thirty kilometers away, just inside Turkey's border with Armenia, its conical-shaped mass filled the horizon.

We traveled on to Erzurum and then north to the Black Sea, where we decided to book passage on a small Turkish cruise ship to Istanbul. We caught up to the ship at Samsun and went aboard. The accommodation was wonderfully comfortable. After dinner each night, waiters served dessert and coffee in the lounge while musicians performed. To us it seemed the height of luxury.

The ship made lengthy stops at Zonguldak and Sinop, and we went ashore. In the latter city, some children tossed stones at us, as we wandered through an old residential neighborhood, reminding us of similar experiences in Iran. This practice, the roots of which I still do not fully understand, was obviously widespread. I wondered if it was because they thought we were Christians and/or because they knew we were outsiders. Or was it for some other reason altogether?[1]

Sailing down the Bosphorus to Istanbul at daybreak was delightful. At that time, no bridges from the European to the Asian side marred the view. And, of course, the city was much smaller

---

[1] Historian Samuel Eliot Morison found that such a practice also existed in Marblehead, Massachusetts, during colonial times. Showers of stones sometimes greeted strangers to that community. "Elbridge Gerry, Gentleman-Democrat," New England Quarterly, 2 (1929), 9.

than it is today, with many fewer tall buildings on the hillsides along the waterway.

After a few days sightseeing, we traveled south to Izmir, planning to take a ferry across the Aegean Sea to Athens. We discovered, however, that travel by water had been stopped between the two countries, supposedly because there had been an outbreak of hoof and mouth disease in Turkey. The two neighbors had a long history of sniping at each other in this way. We made our way north to the border crossing in Thrace. Arriving late at night in a raging storm, we found the border closed there as well.

We decided to return to Izmir and fly from there to the Greek capital. For some reason, flights were allowed. Purchasing airline tickets for $160 was not an expense we had built into our very slim budget. We spent no more than US$15 each day for the two of us. That included food, accommodation and transportation. It seems preposterous today. Of course, the further west we went in Europe, the more difficult it was to stick to the budget.

While waiting for the flight several days hence, we traveled down to the Mediterranean coast at Bodrum. It was then still a small, pleasant town. Even though it was mid-October, I swam each day. A tourist ship from Rhodes appeared one afternoon, and a pop-up shop on the dock began selling duty-free foreign liquor and cigarettes to the tourists who came ashore. I was excited and purchased a bottle of scotch. The clerk asked me what my cabin number was, so it could be delivered later on board. I froze momentarily, but recovered quickly, saying, "I have to have it now!" Reluctantly, he handed it over.

Finally, we caught our short flight to Athens and reunion with the Halls. It was so good to see them both again. Barry was now Australian ambassador to Greece, and we stayed in the great comfort of the residence. During that time, we did not pay much attention to the fact that Greece was still being ruled by the harsh military dictatorship that had come to power in 1967.

We ended up spending three memorable weeks in the country. We visited Crete and many sites on the mainland including Delphi and Meteora. At the Byzantine ruins near Mystras in the Peloponnesus, we met an older Greek man who had worked for many years in Australia. When I asked him how much the bus fare was to the nearby town, he answered in his rusty English, "half-past eight drachmas."

We left Greece in early November by train for Venice. It was getting quite cold in the Italian city. Nevertheless, we visited all the major tourist sites. I remember standing in front of the big windows of an expensive restaurant one evening, watching diners consume delicious looking meals and rich desserts. We would have presented quite a sight to those on the inside if anyone had looked our way.

Then, on to Switzerland, where my old friend Alta Townes was teaching in an exclusive private girls' school near Montreux. She had served as a Peace Corps Volunteer in Shiraz, and we had worked together in Tuyserkan during the summer training program in 1969. It was good to see her again. She had obtained dining privileges for us in the school dining hall, and we welcomed her thoughtfulness. We enjoyed walks along the shores of Lake Geneva and long talks with Alta.

By mid-November we were in London, where we spent two weeks before our departure for Australia. We had a wonderful reunion with Sheena and also with Brian Street, Andre Singer and Teresa Huntley. There were other friends of Ginny's whom I met for the first time. The weather in London was pretty grim. The air was still quite polluted. Days were short; we barely saw the sun. We ate mostly in ethnic restaurants, Cypriot, Greek, Italian, Indian, trying to avoid British fare, which in those days tended to be heavy and not particularly appetizing.

When December 1 arrived, we were ready to leave. We had scheduled four days in Bangkok and then on to Sydney at last. Students had protested against the military takeover in Thailand recently, and when we arrived, bullet holes still pockmarked the walls downtown. We witnessed no disturbances ourselves, and the time passed quickly in sightseeing and one short train trip out of the capital to Ayudhya, an important historical site. I can remember marveling at all the brightly colored vegetables and fruits on display in the open-air market, only a few of which I could recognize.

Ginny had been abroad for almost three years, and she was excited at the thought of seeing her parents again and of having them meet me. I looked forward to our first meeting. I knew all would go well if I could win over the Dixons' quirky little Australian Terrier, Sam. I had heard enough about him to know that it would take every ounce of charm to win him over. We flew down the coast to the small country town of Moruya. Once we left Sydney, the small plane passed low over hundreds of kilometers of largely empty white beaches with pounding surf. To the right stretched as far as I could see the beautiful eucalyptus forests for which Australia was famous.[2]

We spent several days at Tuross Head, resting and getting to know each other. Sam accepted my presence; we actually got on quite well. With Ginny's parents, I talked a good deal about possible teaching positions, as the new school year was less than two months away. Edward Dixon had been immensely helpful suggesting people to contact in and around Sydney.

We left, promising to return for Christmas, when hopefully the employment question would have been resolved, and we could relax more. In Sydney I had several interviews and finally accepted a position at the Convent of the Sacred Heart School in Elizabeth Bay. This private girls' school was located right on Sydney Harbor and had a sister school at Rose Bay to which we would move in a year's time.

I had never considered teaching in a private school, but I could not work in government schools because I did not have teaching credentials, even though I had been teaching and training teachers for over five years. At Elizabeth Bay, I would teach upper-level geography and economics. The state government set the curriculum for all schools.

That first year went by quickly. We found an apartment in Woollahra in Sydney's Eastern Suburbs. I could walk to work from there. I worked hard to master the material, which was much more advanced than what was taught in US high schools. The effort paid off, and my senior geography students performed very well on the Higher School Certificate exam at the end of the year. The headmaster, who was also a geographer, was a great support. We were all expected to participate in some extracurricular activity, so I began a camera club complete with darkroom.

By the middle of 1974, we had begun to think about a trip during the long recess in December-January. At first, we considered travel in Australia, but that would be expensive. So, we thought, why spend that much here when for the same amount we could travel overseas. So, we looked at Southeast Asia.

One day when I got home, Ginny told me excitedly that she had found a relatively inexpensive fare to Kabul. From there we could travel on easily to Iran. Perhaps her thinking had been influ-

---

[2] This was the same area that would experience such terrible bushfires in fall 2019.

enced by a letter we received about that time from Fatimeh. An American friend, for whom our former maid worked part time, had written her words in English. It was largely a formal, flowery piece, but it touched us deeply that she would take the time and that she remembered us so fondly. She had written in part, "I miss you and even though you are far from me you are in my thoughts always. When you left, I was in a bad state for ten days, then gradually, I became well, but I still think of you. When I go to the Holy Haram of Imam Reza, I always pray for you first, and I hope God will bless you."

And so it came to pass. We were going back to Iran. Clearly, it still exerted a strong pull on our emotions. I am sure the Dixons thought we were crazy, but they said nothing. We left in mid-December, flying a circuitous route to Kabul. The ticket was for forty-five days and required that we spend any time after January 1, 1975, in South Asia. Thus, our days in Iran would be limited.

We took the bus route from Kabul through Afghanistan to Herat, where we had a brief reunion with Ahmad, then on to Mashhad. Tom Gordon was still teaching for the university, but many former friends had departed. We stayed at Tom's lovely old home for a few days, seeing whomever we could. Unfortunately, Fatimeh had gone to stay with her family in the village. We saw Josie, who hardly paid us any attention. She had bonded with the Frasers.

We took the train to Tehran, staying there only overnight. That was long enough for me to notice an unexpected surliness aimed at us by Iranian passersby in the bus depot area of the capital. I did not pay a lot of attention to it then, but in retrospect it might have indicated growing tensions.

We had decided to visit the Bashiris again in Ghasr-e Shirin, where the weather would be warm. Mr. Ehsani traveled down from Marivan to see us. I enjoyed this reunion with two of my best friends.

I decided not to return to Tuyserkan. In December, the roads could be bad. More importantly, I worried that it might be too much of an emotional strain to go back to my old town.

Instead, we returned to Mashhad and spent a few more days with Tom. It was the Christmas season so there was quite a bit of socializing within the expatriate community. As required, we crossed back into Afghanistan on January 1, wondering if it had all been worthwhile. But on reflection we thought it had been, for in addition to seeing close friends, we both felt even more certain that we had made the right decision to leave the previous year.

Many former volunteers would return to work in Iran during the last years of the shah's reign. American companies were offering good salaries to those who knew the country and the language. But the expatriate life no longer attracted us.

In Herat we said goodbye to Ahmad. We did not see him again. I do not know what happened to him and his family when all the troubles came to his country in the second half of the 1970s and beyond. He had an uncle in Frankfurt, who owned a carpet shop. Ahmad sometimes brought him new stock. I like to think that he went there, but he also loved his city, so he might have stayed on through the turmoil.

We often reflect on the sad fact that much of the old land route from India to Europe that we travelled so happily, is now closed to tourists. Until the late seventies, one could roam leisurely from one country to another, but then, one by one, they each became embroiled in violence. Although one might visit a single country such as Iran as we would do in 2003, it had become too dangerous to follow the old overland route.

We spent the rest of our holiday in India and Nepal, neither of which I had visited previously. Ginny had passed briefly through India on her Indiaman trip in 1967. We traveled first to Agra to see the magnificent Taj Mahal and other royal tombs and palaces of the Mughal dynasty (1526-1720 CE). I was amazed at how similar the architecture and ornamentation were to structures in Iran. Clearly, the Safavids had left a strong impression on the Muslim rulers of India. There were, of course, features unique to the subcontinent. For example, I had never seen inlaid semiprecious stones as in the wall decoration of the Taj Mahal.

We visited Fatehpur Sikri, the short-lived capital of the Mughal Empire built by Akbar the Great in 1571. The magnificent buildings stood empty except for a reciter of the Qur'an and his students in one of the courtyards. We immediately recognized this activity, which was commonly seen in mosques throughout Iran.

In Varanasi, Khajuraho, and Katmandu any Iranian influence disappeared. Hindu symbols appeared everywhere. I found it difficult in the short time available to interpret this art with which I had little familiarity.

Everywhere we saw poverty that far surpassed what we had witnessed in Iran. One night in Bombay as we sat at a garden table, beggars cried out imploringly for alms, as they stretched their long arms through the tall hedge that separated the restaurant from the sidewalk beyond.

As our trip came to a close, and we headed back to Sydney, we reflected on the fact that our travels were always characterized by constant movement from one place to another. We never stopped for long anywhere. One day, we agreed, we should go to a single location and spend the entire holiday in that vicinity.

During the next several years, we had few occasions to draw on our joint knowledge of Iran. There were then few Iranians in Sydney, and Australians were not particularly interested in our Middle Eastern experiences. Debates over domestic politics and the sacking of Prime Minister Gough Whitlam in 1975 took center stage.

We also welcomed the births of our sons, Matthew (1975) and Zachary (1977). Between parenting, work, socializing with family and friends and some coursework, our days seemed very full. We did not pay a lot of attention to what was happening in Iran.

Presenting Iran and the Middle East

Now a family of four, we returned to the United States in summer 1978, so I could study for a doctorate in history. I had considered a graduate degree in TEFL at the University of Minnesota, but Indiana University offered me a reasonably good package to study history in Bloomington. It turned out to be an excellent choice. Not only was the program a strong one with two of the foremost scholars of the history of US foreign relations, Robert H. Ferrell and David M. Pletcher, on the faculty, but the town proved to be a wonderful place for children. This would be our home for the next six years.

We had enjoyed our four-and-a-half years in Australia, and we were sad to say good-bye to family and friends. I had learned much about good teaching at the Convent of the Sacred Heart and in my Diploma of Education classes. But now I realized it was time to leave if I were ever to earn a PhD. The longer I waited the more difficult would be the transition from teacher to student. Ginny agreed, although the decision to distance herself once again from her family did not come easily.

By the time we got settled in Bloomington in mid-August, daily news reports from Iran were indicating that domestic unrest had become worse than we could have imagined. Even then, however, we had difficulty believing that the shah would be overthrown. He had weathered earlier crises, especially in 1953 and 1962. He had gained much experience and possessed a formidable military. Of course, we knew nothing of what was happening behind the scenes, the shah's health deteriorating rapidly, disaffection spreading throughout the lower ranks in the armed forces, the effectiveness of the network of religious and secular opponents within Iran and abroad.

My classes were extremely demanding, and I worked two part-time jobs as well, so I did not have time to dwell on day-to-day events in Iran. Whenever I came up for air, however, stories of ominous developments in Iran continued to fill the newspapers and the TV news. We wondered throughout that period how our friends in Tuyserkan and Mashhad were managing. Unfortunately, we had lost touch with them since our last visit at the end of 1974.

Yet, in academic life, Iran soon came back into focus for me and in an unexpected way. My dissertation director, Robert Ferrell, suggested that I focus on United States relations with Iran since the end of World War II. He thought it was an excellent fit given my particular experience and ability to use Persian sources. He was absolutely correct. I should have understood this earlier.

As Iran descended into revolution, the Hostage Crisis unfolded, and the Iran-Iraq War began, more and more books and articles appeared focusing on aspects of the US-Iran relationship. Many of these were ill-informed, written by individuals who had little if any firsthand experience of the country and its people. I knew I could make an important contribution; I could bring a degree of internal understanding along with an outsider's perspective to my work. This combination would serve as a small counterweight to what was becoming in academia and elsewhere the demonization of Iran and its people.

One of the American diplomats held hostage, was John Limbert, a former Peace Corps Volunteer in Sanandaj and a staff member of several PC training programs. He and his Iranian wife, Parvaneh, helped train our group in 1968. John became a friend, and I could only imagine how conflicted he must have been when the Iranians he loved took him hostage. Even after that ordeal, he has never stopped advocating for improvement in bilateral relations.

One of the greatest surprises came in February 1979, when I happened to see the picture of my old Georgetown acquaintance, Sadegh, on the front cover of a national news magazine. Soon, he was everywhere. Sadegh Ghotbzadeh, it appeared, was one of Ayatollah Khomaini's closest advisers and had returned to Tehran with him on the Air France flight on February 1. After his visa had been suspended during the Johnson administration, Sadegh had gone to Europe and the Middle East to work for fifteen years with student groups and others in opposition to the shah. Now his efforts were being rewarded, and he was at the center of revolutionary developments in Tehran.[3]

How did it all go so wrong, the shah's bid to transform Iran, the American plan to make the shah a pillar of strength in the region? These and similar questions became the focus of my scholarship over the ensuing years. As I pored over government records here and abroad, I gradually uncovered a complex picture of the rise and fall of Mohammad Reza Pahlavi.

During those first years at graduate school, I began to attend academic conferences, especially those of the Middle East Studies Association and the International Society for Iranian Studies. Many Iranian Americans came as well, and there were sharp divisions in those early years between the supporters of the old regime and those who supported the revolution. I watched this drama unfold as an onlooker. I did not have close friends in either camp, nor was I drawn to a single ideological persuasion. I found it painful, however, to see many academics tossing aside careful analysis to score political points. I had witnessed this same sad phenomenon among American scholars of the Cold War.

Nearer to home, I had the opportunity to attend an Azeri-Turkish conference held in Bloomington shortly after our arrival. During the time of the shah, this large minority had faced restrictions to teaching and using their language in the schools and in publishing books in their native language. They wanted to ensure that the new government in Tehran did not try to re-impose those controls. I sympathized with their demands. At one point in the discussion, seizing a rare opportunity to use my language skills, I asked a question in Persian, which most of the attendees understood. I do not remember the question, but I do recall the response. Members of the audience shouted me down, yelling out that only Turkish should be used, and if not that, then English. Persian was not to be tolerated.

---

[3] Ghotbzadeh served as foreign minister, 1979-1980. Accused of plotting a coup against the regime, he was imprisoned and executed at Evin prison in September 1982.

I am sure I was in a minority of Americans, rooting, as I did, for Iran in the conflict initiated by Saddam Hussein. I knew that he viewed Iranians as the primordial enemies of the Arab nation. Once in an Egyptian bookstore, I purchased a bundle of the Iraqi leader's brief essays on a variety of topics. Two of these had revealing titles: *A Spotlight on Syrian-Iranian Collusion* (1982) and *Thus We Should Fight Persians* (1983). He argued that Ayatollah Khomaini had started the hostilities.

The war lasted eight years and took a frightful toll on the population of both countries. Missiles fired at Iranian cities caused many civilian casualties. Friends in Malayer in western Iran told me that they had moved to the countryside during the war years to escape random missile attacks. Then, too, Iraq used poison gas against Iranian soldiers with deadly effect.

I remember visiting the Isfahan bazaar many years later and being shown sites where missiles had landed, resulting in considerable destruction. In Isfahan also, we encountered a large group of teenage girls from Mazandaran. They were "daughters of martyrs" in the war. A government agency organized and chaperoned them on periodic trips to historical and cultural sites around the country.

While all these events were unfolding, I was working on my dissertation on US-Iran relations in the early postwar years. I had the opportunity to translate many Persian newspapers and journal articles from those days. I became especially interested in the career of Mohammad Musaddiq. I came to view him as a hero. I tried to remain objective in my analysis, but there was just so much to admire about the man, whom the CIA had helped to overthrow in August 1953.

My dissertation became a book, and other books would follow. Nevertheless, finding a permanent academic position in the early 1980s was not easy. I accepted a three-year contract at the University of Georgia in Athens. This was exciting. I had never lived in the Deep South. Everyone in the history department welcomed us in a friendly manner. I had no opportunity, of course, to teach anything other than introductory US history courses.

Ginny had worked part-time at Indiana University Press, so it was natural that she would accept a job at the University of Georgia Press. She has often remarked that it was one of the best positions she ever had. She made many friends and learned a great deal about publishing in the short time she was there.

Our sons went to Oglethorpe Elementary, a really fine public school with dedicated teachers. I assumed the school had only recently been integrated. African Americans made up half of the student body. Bonnie London served as principal, and she proved to be an excellent administrator. She had such a nurturing manner, but she could make hard decisions also. The children, including our own, thought she was grand.

In the nature of short-term academic appointments, one is obliged to begin searching for something more permanent from day one, no time to relax. The history chair at UGA told us that under no circumstance could our contracts be extended beyond the three-year period. So, the hunt continued.

How many job applications did I send out? I lost count. I had a successful interview—I thought—at the American Historical Association Conference in New York City in January 1986, but apparently nothing came of that. More than two-and-a-half months went by, and I had heard nothing after that talk with the representative from Grand Valley State College in Allendale, Michigan. I assumed the job had gone to someone else, and they had just neglected to inform me. Then in mid-March, I received an urgent phone call from Dennis Devlin, who had interviewed me earlier. Could I come as soon as possible for an on-campus meeting, he asked. Although it was an unusually long time since New York City, I speedily agreed.

Only much later, long after I had accepted the job at GVSC, did I learn what had transpired over that two-and-a-half-month period. A tug of war had taken place between the history department, which had a favored, inside candidate, and the dean, Forrest Armstrong, who held the department's feet to the fire. The advertisement for the position asked for someone who could teach courses on the non-Western world or the Third World as it was often called. The department's candidate could not. Thus, said the dean, he was ineligible, and they must look elsewhere. That was when the frantic call went out to Athens, Georgia.

The dean was impressed with my Peace Corps experience and the teaching I had done abroad. I fit the requirements of the position and had the strong endorsement of Dr. Devlin. The department offered me the job. Clearly, my work in Iran had helped secure the tenure-track position. I happily remained at Grand Valley for thirty-two years.

And so, after only two years in Georgia, we moved yet again, this time permanently. In the mid-1980s West Michigan seemed very homogeneous in regard to its population. It was largely white with a predominance of Dutch Calvinists, especially in the small towns. We settled in Grand Haven on the shores of Lake Michigan. When the boys started school, they were surprised that there were almost no students of color in their classes nor indeed in the entire school. Their schools both in Bloomington, Indiana, and Athens, Georgia, had students of diverse races and ethnicities. Just before our first Martin Luther King Jr. Day in Michigan in January 1987, my younger son asked his fourth-grade teacher if they would be celebrating the day. His answer, "No, there are no black students in our class."

Even at the college, a certain traditional narrowness prevailed. The curriculum reflected this. There were virtually no non-Western courses in our department, and this was the same in most other departments in the Arts and Humanities Division. A number of administrators and faculty, however, wanted to encourage changes, to make the curriculum represent new developments in global history and area studies. Thus, from the outset, I had support in my efforts to internationalize the university in whatever ways possible.[4]

I developed new courses focused on the Middle East and Iran. With the help of colleagues in other departments we established a Middle East Studies program, which I directed for ten years. We set up an annual Model Arab League simulation for interested students, which still continues after thirty-three years. I also organized study abroad programs to Egypt, Morocco, and Turkey for interested students. We invited Middle Eastern scholars to lecture on campus, many of whom focused on Iran. Scholars such as Nasrin Rahimieh, Sheila Blair, and filmmaker, Bahman Farmanara, became good friends.

I received many invitations to speak about Iran and Islam in schools and churches in the region. Those sessions were some of the most rewarding of my teaching career. We organized workshops on the Middle East for area teachers, who would take the information we provided into their own classrooms. These were all wonderful developments and over the years and with the support of many colleagues, the curriculum and the university programs were transformed. I like to think Dean Armstrong got his money's worth.

---

[4] GVSC became GVSU in 1987.

The Iranian revolution had a strange impact on the trajectory of my career. Although I continued to research and write on Iran, there were now barriers to easy movement between the United States and Iran. This was especially true when undergraduate students were involved. To accommodate both my own research interests and the needs of our students, it became necessary to move beyond Iran. Very soon, I became engaged with the Arab and Turkish worlds. I doubt this would have happened if Iran had remained easily accessible as in the pre-revolutionary days.

I traveled in Arab countries for the first time, including Egypt, Syria, Jordan, Palestine, Lebanon, and Morocco. I came to see the great similarities with Iran but also to appreciate the significant differences.

In Cairo I made a point of visiting the tomb of the late shah, who had died in the Egyptian capital in 1980. Like his father before him, he had been laid to rest among the deceased kings of Egypt in the Al-Rifa'i Mosque. The grave had become a pilgrimage site for Iranian royalists, and I visited it whenever I was in the capital to see what tokens of esteem they might have left behind. Once, I discovered a single red rose lying on the engraved white marble stone. On another occasion, I found an eloquent poem of atonement, the last stanza of which read,

> O Lord, give us all the strength and perseverance to
> rise above our pettiness and look beyond to a better
> future for all Iranians. I offer these prayers to my
> late King: "May your soul rest in peace. May you look
> over us and forgive our sins against you and help us
> bring about goodness, kindness, compassion and light
> back to our ravaged and darkened homeland, Iran."[5]

I spent a good deal of time in Turkey as well, teaching there as a Fulbrighter in 1999-2000. The upper-middle class students I taught at very secular Bilkent University in Ankara feared that the Ayatollahs were coming to take over their country. Only with great difficulty was I able to discuss with them the origins and develop-

---

[5] After his death in South Africa in 1944, Reza Shah had been temporarily buried in Al-Rifa'i Mosque. His body was disinterred in 1951 and returned to Iran to be reburied in a splendid mausoleum in Rey just outside Tehran.

ment of the revolution in neighboring Iran, for they resisted any balanced consideration of what had happened there.

I will never forget one day during office hours, a student, who slipped into my office and closed the door behind him. He told me that he was a scholarship student and also deeply religious. He had welcomed the discussion about Iran, he told me, but he could never express his views to his secular classmates; if he did, he could not remain on campus. I immediately saw the irony of his situation; he was being intimidated into silence by secular liberals, who were busily accusing the Islamic radicals of having the same effect on their opponents.

As my familiarity with the region grew, I saw also the common problems that these countries faced. Nevertheless, they rarely cooperated. Iranians often made rude comments about Arabs and Turks. The former, they said, were "lizard eaters". The Arabs reciprocated. Once in East Jerusalem in 1969, I proudly mentioned to a local shopkeeper that we were living and working in Iran. He made a disparaging remark, showing no interest whatsoever in discussing life in Iran. As for the Turks, they often made rude comments about the Arabs, fewer, perhaps, about the Iranians. One day I was waiting for the train with some of my Bilkent students and the subject of Arabs arose. A bright young female student launched into a tirade against them, claiming they were backward and ate with their fingers. I doubt that she had ever met an Arab.

Over the years at scholarly conferences, the Middle East Studies Conference, for example, I have observed that members of various diaspora communities, Turks, Arabs, Iranians, and even Kurds, tend to stick together. Rarely, do members of one ethnic group turn up at presentations by members of another. There are, I imagine, a number of reasons why this happens, but I have always believed that this traditional separation makes for a less vibrant intellectual community.

I wrote a book, *Negotiating for the Past* (2008), which focuses on the history of archaeology in the Middle East between the two world wars. This study underscores the similarities I mentioned above. It all began when I was working in the diplomatic records at the National Archives in Washington, and I came across multiple cross-references to "Persepolis," the ancient Iranian site outside Shiraz. I wondered what Persepolis could possibly have to do with foreign relations. I made a note to return later to try to answer that question. When I came back a few years later, I discovered that controversies over archaeological sites were at the center of US-Iran relations in the interwar years. I researched this topic in a number of archives here and abroad.

Later, I began to take students for study-abroad trips to Egypt, and slowly I gathered material there about the interaction of Western archaeologists, American diplomats, and Egyptian nationalists as I had already done for Iran. The similarities were astounding.

Then I taught at Bilkent University, and while there, I collected information on the same topic wherever I could. Once again, the interactions in early Republican Turkey looked quite like what its neighbors had experienced. Finally, I added Iraq because the Oriental Institute's rich archives at the University of Chicago, where I did much research, featured a number of excavations and interactions with nationalists in Baghdad.

When I ended, I had four case studies, each of which repeated a remarkably similar story of how these forces, archaeologists, diplomats, and nationalists, came into conflict with each other during those pivotal years. The names of the countries seemed almost interchangeable. My hope was that anyone reading the book would understand that what happened in one of these countries happened in all of them. That they shared common problems, past and present, and should perhaps seek common solutions.

Cut off from Iran itself in the early years of the revolution, I grasped at any opportunity to reconnect with Iranians. When I visited Syria in summer 1994, I had several experiences with Iranians in Damascus, all of them unplanned and unexpected. Many pilgrims came to visit the Sayyidah Zaynab Mosque, the burial place according to Twelver Shia belief of the sister of Imam Hussein, daughter of Ali and granddaughter of the Prophet. The Iranian government had spent a great sum to restore and refurbish the shrine, all in the Iranian style with the use of richly colored ceramic tiles throughout. When I visited, there were many pilgrims, and a *rowza* or mourning ceremony was taking place, with recitations, wailing and tears. There were also many pilgrims at the Umayyad Mosque at the spot where the severed head of Imam Hussein had temporarily rested centuries earlier.

Later, in the city, I talked to a member of a large group of pilgrims from Kerman, preparing to return to Iran on a Mahan Air flight. He told me that they did not need a visa to visit Syria. He owned a taxi service at home and reported that everything had become expensive. They had not brought carpets to sell, only pistachios.

Another group had come overland by bus through Turkey. The driver of one bus told me it took two-and-a-half days to reach the Iranian border from Damascus, and pilgrims paid US$30.00 for a one-way ticket from Tehran. They also brought carpets to sell in the *souk* (Arab marketplace) to defray the cost of the journey. He volunteered that his married daughter lived in Los Angeles and that he had visited her there several times.

The shops in the *souk* displayed a lot of small, reasonably inexpensive Iranian carpets, but the shopkeepers did not welcome Iranians. One told me he had to learn a little Persian in order to keep them out of his shop and to get them to leave if they came in. They seemed to wander through the narrow passageways as if in a daze. From their dress, I surmised that many of them were of humble origin. This might have been their first trip outside Iran.

In the main square of Damascus, the Islamic Republic had set up the Iranian Cultural Center, which sold Iranian products. It also handed out published material mainly in Arabic. I looked for a Persian speaker, but the workers I met spoke only Arabic.

All this, of course, was long before the civil war in Syria, when Iran became engaged militarily in the struggle to save the regime of Bashar al-Assad. But as Saddam Hussein had charged in 1982, the Syrians had already abandoned their brother Arabs to join forces with the despised Persians. That alliance has lasted to the present.

Seeing for Ourselves

Our opportunity to return to Iran finally came almost a decade after my chance encounters in Syria. The presidency of Mohammad Khatami provided a more welcoming environment for scholarly exchange. In fall 2002, I applied for a senior fellowship from the American Institute of Iranian Studies (AIIS) in New York City. Happily, I received the grant, and I applied to Tehran University to sponsor my visit and help me obtain a visa. That was a long process, taking months, but finally by summer 2003, everything was in place.

Ginny's path to obtaining a visa is worth recounting. She applied in early summer to the Iranian Interests Section at the Embassy of Pakistan in Washington. She knew that she did not have a lot of time, so when she spoke to the Iranian official, she told him the story of how we had met and married in Tehran, about our life in

Mashhad and finally related how much we both loved his country. He was very sympathetic. She received her visa in three weeks.

While all our travel arrangements were being finalized, I received an unexpected invitation to present a lecture at Cal Poly State University in San Luis Obispo, California. It would commemorate the fiftieth anniversary of the 1953 overthrow of Mohammad Musaddiq. I had recently published a book entitled, *The US and Iran: In the Shadow of Musaddiq* (1997), hence the invitation. The city and the natural beauty of its surroundings captivated us, and eventually, we would retire to this Central Coast community. You could say, without too much exaggeration, that Musaddiq had led us to our new home.

Our trip to Iran was not a simple undertaking because President Bush in early 2002 had included Iran along with Iraq and North Korea in the so-called Axis of Evil. This astounded anyone who knew how helpful Iran had been in the campaign against the Taliban in Afghanistan. To designate Iran in this way seemed to defy all reason. The State Department website carried numerous warnings to any American citizen foolish enough to consider traveling to Iran. Anyone who read that and had no previous experience with Iran, would surely have turned away. We persisted.

I planned to visit a number of archaeological sites spread around the country. Some I had visited previously. Persepolis, for example, figured hugely in the study I was writing. I was approaching them all from a totally different perspective than when I had served as a Peace Corps Volunteer. Now, I was particularly interested in the history of excavation and the role of such sites in the collective consciousness of the nation.

I decided that I would need a driver and a car to reach all these locations within the two-and-a-half weeks we would be in Iran. I made the arrangements from the States, paying in advance through a bank in Spain. This was still possible as US sanctions on Iran were limited.

Ginny would have to wear hijab throughout our stay, so we paid a visit to shops in the Arab-American community of Dearborn, Michigan. She bought a floor-length coat that fully covered her from the neck down. Unfortunately, the heavy material was far from ideal for an Iranian summer.

We departed July 18, from Chicago on Turkish Airlines. We planned to spend a few days on each end of our trip in Istanbul, a city we both loved. While we were having dinner at an outdoor restaurant located right along the street in the old city center of Sultanahmet, our waiter asked what brought us to Turkey. We told him that we were on our way to Iran for a few weeks. With that, he proudly announced that an Iranian family was staying in the small hotel just across the street. He had waited on them a day earlier. As we got up to leave after our meal, he came running over to us to point out that the Iranians were just coming out the door of the hotel. What a coincidence.

We started a conversation with the family, a mother, two daughters and one American boyfriend. The older daughter and her boyfriend lived in Los Angeles, the younger daughter had come with her mother to see her sister, who had been abroad for several years. The younger daughter, Sara, was waiting for her US visa to arrive from the embassy in Dubai (In those years, Iranians could apply for a US visa only in Dubai or Ankara.) She was getting nervous as she should have already received it. She had been accepted to study electrical engineering at Western Michigan University in Kalamazoo, which was about seventy-five miles from our home in Grand Haven—another amazing coincidence. Sara and her mother were about to set off for the two-day bus trip back to Tehran. They insisted we contact them when we arrived.

We landed in Tehran in the wee hours of the morning of Monday, July 21, twenty-eight years since our last visit. How had Iran changed, we wondered? Would we still love it the way we once had?

One reality had not changed, although we arrived at 4:00 a.m., Mehrabad Airport was packed. As we moved slowly through customs, I noticed that women were dressed in a variety of clothing, some of it seemed more revealing than I expected. Perhaps, Ginny's dress would prove too conservative.

On the flight, there had been no loud prayers shouted out either in taking off or landing, even though most passengers were Iranian. In the old days one always heard such prayers for safe travels. As soon as we crossed into Iran, the women on board began to cover up. Many were watching Ginny to see what she would do. She, too, put on her long coat and head scarf.

Our driver, Asghar Khademi, was waiting and guided us expertly to his car through the gridlock in the parking area. We were relieved when we arrived at the hotel just before sunrise. We said goodbye to Asghar until Saturday.

The heat that summer in Tehran broke records, and we had arrived in the hottest days. Furthermore, the air conditioner in our room was not working properly. This was going to be a challenge.

Later that day, after a few hours' sleep, and with the thermometer showing a sizzling 41°C (106°F), we forced ourselves to go outside to complete some important errands. We registered at the American Interests section at the Swiss Embassy and at the Australian Embassy as well, for Ginny was not yet an American citizen. At one point an Iranian gentleman whispered in my ear, "America is very good!" I thought that was a reassuring welcome.

Next, we went to Iran Doostan, the travel company, to meet with Sholeh, who would finalize the details of our trip. She was extremely helpful. She even located our Tuyserkani friends. I knew that most of the Ehsani family, and other families as well, had moved to Tehran in the intervening years. Sholeh looked through the phonebook; she could find only one Mashollah Ehsani listed. She called, and my old friend answered. How wonderful it was to hear his welcoming voice again. He told Ginny that he knew we would come back. He insisted that we visit them the following day.

Then off to the shops to look for alternative dress for Ginny, who was suffering from the heat. We visited several boutiques, but nothing appealed. We found it ironic that men were working in all these women's shops, usually with a female assistant; yet on the buses men sat at the front, women at the back. Obviously, we had a lot to learn.

The next day, we had more success, and Ginny bought a new *ruh-poosh* (cloak). Then we found a tailor who would alter the one she came with, shortening the length and the arms. He whispered to me as we were leaving that he liked Americans but not the Iranian clerics.

As we became more familiar with dress styles, it became apparent that Iranian women, especially young women, tested the dress codes every day. No one knew exactly where the line was that could not be crossed without repercussions. Many wore shorter coats and pushed their scarves back to reveal more hair. The morality police could challenge them at any time, but they seemed comfortable taking the risk.

We had a great reunion with Ehsani and Mahvash and their daughter's son, Farhad. Mahtab lived nearby, and Farhad had grown close to his grandparents, spending much of his time with them. Ehsani filled us in on all the family. Brother Nasrollah had died a few years earlier, leaving his wife and three grown children. Mansour and Teimour lived in Tehran with their families. Ehsani's sons, Masoud and Saeed, worked in Tehran. Both were married with children. Ghassem Bashiri and his wife, Ashraf, and their children now lived in Kermanshah. They had four children; two additional sons had been born after we left Iran. Sister Aroos and her family had remained in Malayer. Mr. Dabaghi still lived in Tuyserkan.

The Ehsani family had little to do with the revolution. There seemed to be even more corruption than before. I heard this repeatedly during our stay. Under President Khatami, the situation outside the home seemed freer and more relaxed.

After our return from the Ehsanis, Dr. Gholam-Abbas Tavasoli, my host from Tehran University, had come to the hotel to welcome us and to arrange for a meeting with interested faculty the next afternoon. We met with a small group on campus, and I talked about my history of archaeology project. They agreed that the current regime lacked public backing; only those it rewarded supported it. For some reason they wanted me to speak with the man who had translated my earlier book (without permission, of course) on Musaddiq. I did as they requested, and we talked on the telephone. He asked me to sign the Persian copy of the book for him.

The faculty assured me that Iranians liked Americans, but they wondered if the reverse were true. They remarked that President Khatami had been open and friendly toward the United States; the night before he had given a wonderful speech in which he praised Abraham Lincoln. Washington had not responded in kind, they said.

The next day, we visited several museums. Iran Bastan Museum had been built in the 1930s and next door, the Islamic Museum opened in 1996. It contained informative and well-presented exhibits. Later, as we strolled past the foreign ministry, I wanted to take a picture of the mock-Achaemenid entranceway, but a passerby and then two soldiers warned me off. The latter told me if I persisted, they would take my film. Then, we walked to the wall in front of the so-called Nest of Spies, that is, the former US Embassy. Again, I was forbidden to take any photos. One soldier remarked, "If you take a picture, you will go to prison, and if I let you, I will go also." I put away my camera.

Bahman Farminara had become a good friend ever since his visit to GVSU during our annual Middle East film festival, when I had chauffeured him around the area. He was a well-known and successful film director. He came from a wealthy family, which owned textile factories in Iran. He had gone to Canada for a number of years after the revolution, but when his children had grown up and did not need his supervision any longer, he returned. He reestablished his film career under the new regime. When I asked him how he coped with censorship, he said that he always put in several inconsequential items that he knew the censors would immediately object to. When they did, he would remove them, usually leaving intact the essence of the film.

Bahman invited us to his house in Lashkarak to the north of Tehran. His driver picked us up, and we drove for about an hour to reach our destination. The house was full of friends and family celebrating the birthday of a grandson. It was good to see Bahman again. He had wanted us to stay with him, but we had much to do in the city, and his house was too distant from central Tehran.

On the way back, I had a long conversation with the driver. His elder son was about to begin his two years in the army. Apparently, anyone who had enough money could buy his way out of serving. He also told me of caves that had recently been discovered near Hamadan and of some Abbasid excavations at Kashan, which we should check out.[6]

The next evening, we had dinner with a former Alam student, Hadi Navid. Hadi had lived at Tom Gordon's house in Mashhad, and they remained good friends. Hadi had a small publishing firm, and he was a graphic designer as well. He was one of many successful Alam graduates. He took us for dinner to a traditional Iranian restaurant with good music provided by a Kurdish flute and drum. I noticed a number of men wearing ties, which had virtually disappeared during the early years after the revolution when they were considered a sign of Western decadence. What did their reappearance symbolize now, I wondered?

Hadi arranged for us to meet the publisher of my most recent book in translation, which had been done without obtaining permission as was common in Iran. We had lunch with Javad Muzzafar and a Mr. Turkoman, who was a specialist, they said, on Musaddiq. After I signed a copy of the book for him, the publisher gave me fifteen copies for friends. Over lunch Muzzafar revealed that he had

---

[6] The Abbasid Empire began in 750 CE and the Mongols ended it in 1258 CE.

once spent one hundred days in notorious Evin prison for publishing an interview with Ayatollah Montazeri. I assumed it had been critical of Ayatollah Khomaini. Neither the publisher nor the scholar considered Reza Shah to have been a nationalist. I disagreed, suggesting that there was more than one kind of nationalist.[7]

That evening Hadi had arranged a *dooreh* or group meeting of some former Alam students at a restaurant in Abbas Abad, fifteen in all. They had lots of questions, and I signed copies of my book for each of them. These men had done very well in their careers; they were doctors, businessmen, engineers. We enjoyed the evening and the memories.

On 27 July, we set off on the first of two long trips outside Tehran. We would be traveling in the south, where temperatures would easily reach 38°C (100°F) by mid-morning and humidity was high. One had to organize the workday carefully, a few hours early in the morning, a few hours in the late afternoon. Fortunately, bottled water was now available everywhere.

We had arranged that Asghar would meet us at the airport in Ahvaz. I looked forward to seeing him again. He had told us earlier that his family came from Iranian Azerbaijan, and he spoke Azeri Turkish as did millions of Iranians. He was approximately five feet eight inches tall, stocky in build with a mass of black hair. Now forty-three years old, he had served in the Imperial Iranian Navy as a young man. He and his former wife had three children. A married daughter lived in Norway. We would be spending a lot of time together over the next several days, so we would no doubt learn a great deal more about him. Already we sensed that he was gentle yet strong.

Once again on the flight from Tehran to Ahvaz, we heard no loud prayers at either end of the trip. Asghar had driven all the way from Tehran that day, and he was very tired. The plane arrived an hour late, so we would only have time to visit Susa before dark. Unfortunately, we had to scrap plans to go to Chogha Zanbil.[8]

For me, the two most important sites were Susa and Persepolis. I had researched a great deal about their excavations and devoted

---

[7] Ayatollah Montazeri had been the designated successor to Ayatollah Khomaini, but they had a final falling out in 1989 over harsh policies of the regime. After that, Montazeri was banished to Qom.
[8] An Elamite religious center, circa 1250 BCE

many pages to each of them in the manuscript. Any other sites we could visit would be a plus, but those two were essential.

The French had excavated at Susa, an ancient Achaemenid capital, for decades (1885-1938). They had shipped home amazing antiquities, including the Archers Frieze, a multicolored brick decoration from the palace of Darius I (522-486 BCE). I had admired this at the Louvre when I visited there in 1998. The French had also built on the site an impressive walled fort for storing antiquities before shipment and for the safety of the archaeologists in a region still subject until the 1930s to frequent tribal skirmishes. Embedded in the massive walls were pieces of ancient cuneiform tablets and cylinder seals.

Next day, we drove near the major oil fields at Masjid Suleyman and Gachsaran on our way to Bishapur. Oil pipelines stretched in all directions across the landscape, with flaring gas visible at frequent intervals. The average August temperature is 45°C (113°F), and we saw shepherds sheltering under trees, bridges and temporary structures of branches. Young children were finding relief in the occasional water tank.

Asghar related an intriguing tale as we drove along that day. He told us that as a young sailor in the navy, he served on an Iranian vessel in the Persian Gulf. In late summer 1978, they had been tasked, he said, with a top-secret mission, to transport the body of Reza Shah out of the country. I pressed him on this story because if it were accurate, it would indicate that someone in Tehran suspected at an early date that the regime of Mohammad Reza Pahlavi might be in serious trouble. He stuck to his story. Years later, I read that when Reza Shah's tomb in Rey had been destroyed after the revolution, his body had not been found. Rumors abound as to what happened to it. Perhaps, I should have listened more closely to Asghar's tale.

As we moved further inland into the mountains and toward Bishapur, the temperature dropped into the mid-30°C. The Sasanian ruler Shapur I (240-270 CE) had built this now-abandoned city as his capital after defeating the Romans and taking Emperor Valerian (253-260 CE) captive. At the narrow entrance into the valley, he had ordered rock-cut carvings on the towering walls, depicting his great victories. A rushing river flowed the entire length of the valley, and high above the valley floor stood a cave containing a statue of the great ruler. This had collapsed and the last Pahlavi shah had restored it with a suitable plaque attached. For some reason, Asghar did not want to visit the cave, perhaps because of the exertion it would take to get there or because we still had many miles to go before we reached Shiraz. But I insisted. We agreed that I would take myself up the steep, winding path, while he waited below, drinking tea and relaxing on a raised platform in front of a villager's adobe home. The folks here were members of the Qashqa'i people and spoke a dialect of Turkish as did Asghar, so they could talk together in their mother tongue while I climbed.

One path led almost straight upward for about one mile to the mouth of the cave. Ginny came with me about a third of the way and then decided to wait at that spot for my return. Hamad, a teen-age village boy, who suddenly appeared, joined me for the rest of the climb. He fancied himself a guide, and he took the most direct route; I would have preferred a bit of a zigzag. It took over an hour to reach our goal, but it was well worth the effort. The cave was deep and cool. Set in the middle was the huge statue, perhaps ten feet tall. I took many pictures inside and from the entrance looking out over the fertile valley surrounded by mountains.

The trip down took much less time. Hamad told me that approximately thirty foreigners made this hike to the cave each year. I gave him a generous tip for his time, and we said goodbye and rejoined Asghar. The village couple insisted we accept their hospitality, drink tea and rest a bit, and we agreed. What a lovely spot they had. As we were leaving, the woman kissed Ginny's hands, a traditional gesture of courtesy and respect.

It was getting dark as we set off on the winding mountain road, which would bring us back up to the plateau and Shiraz. Asghar was a good driver, but aggressive. On this busy one-lane road, he could not resist weaving in and out of the big trucks and buses that made their way slowly up the pass. The only light relief came when we pulled in behind a lumbering lorry with cartoon pictures of Charlie Chaplin staring at us from the tailgate. We arrived in the famous City of Roses and Nightingales late in the evening.

The next morning, we wandered around the Narenjestan Garden. In one building we came across the offices of eight NGOs, one of which was dedicated to protecting children's rights. We collected samples of their attractively designed literature in Persian. I noticed a billboard along the roadway, which read: "The Authority of the Faqih is the Same as that of the Prophet Mohammad." I wondered how many Iranians believed this.[9]

I had arranged to meet for lunch with Dr. Sarvestani, who was the head of an NGO dedicated to protecting and preserving the culture of Fars Province. He was warm, friendly and polite with a good sense of humor. We had a long discussion about my project during lunch and continuing back at his office. He arranged for us to meet an archaeologist at Persepolis when we visited there the next day. After we had become a little more relaxed with each other, he remarked that Iran did not need the United States and that Washington could certainly not bring democracy to his country, that must come from within. When I asked him where the current Musaddiq was, he replied, "We are waiting."

Later, we continued touring the city, including the Bagh-e Eram and the tomb of Hafiz, the great 14th century Iranian poet. Asghar wanted us to visit the Shah-Cheragh Mosque, a sacred site, but the gatekeeper would not let us in, saying he had orders from above. While Asghar negotiated, an elderly Iranian came up to me and started a conversation. He said he had served in Israel under the old regime. The "good old days," he called them. I was getting nervous as onlookers gathered around us, but he paid them no attention. Finally, I excused myself and the three of us quickly departed.

The next day we visited Persepolis, one of the grandest sites in Iran. We met with Dr. Maziar Kazemi, whom Dr. Sarvestani had recommended. He showed us a new video of the ancient capital, which had not yet been released. It presented the history of the site, but there was not a single word about the many foreign archaeologists who had excavated there in earlier times.

We practically had the whole place to ourselves. We encountered only a handful of foreign tourists, mostly from Spain, and no other Americans, and a few Iranians. I asked Asghar to find out why the Iranians were visiting Persepolis. A mullah admitted that he brought his students to practice their English with foreign tourists. Some girls said they came for recreation. No one talked about the ancient Iranian glories associated with Takht-e Jamshid, as Iranians referred to the site.

We could see more faded glory on the plain just at the foot of the site. There stood the tattered remnants of the shah's glorious

---

[9] A term referring to the Supreme Leader in Iran, originally Ayatollah Khomaini and since 1989, Ayatollah Khamenei.

tent city that the Halls had visited during the great imperial celebrations of October 1971. The phrase, *sic transit gloria mundi*, came to mind.

We stopped at Naqsh-e Rustam to view the hillside tombs of Achaemenid rulers and then at Pasagardae, where the tomb of Cyrus the Great was located. Unfortunately, it was covered in scaffolding and closed to the public. Then, we set off on the long road to Isfahan, our last stop of the day.

Wherever we traveled in Iran, we noticed that many new, broad highways had been built. These tied the distant parts of the country to the capital. In most big cities, however, the crush of traffic was so great, that even with the new roads, congestion often left us sitting in long lines of traffic.

I quote from my diary as we approached Isfahan,

> Traffic coming into the city was terrible. I felt like I had a front row seat to a Schwarzenegger film. Five lanes of traffic on a two-lane road is not uncommon. No braking for pedestrians. Asghar just heads for a group on a crosswalk, expecting them to disappear, and somehow, they do. Motorbikes with one to five passengers (occasionally as many as seven) routinely weave in and out of traffic. This might be the perfect metaphor for the country as a whole, everyone flouts the regulations, but somehow it works.

Like all of Iran's cities, Isfahan had grown almost beyond recognition. The population was now over one and a half million, three times its size in 1972. At the core of the city, however, I quickly recognized the familiar landmarks from the Safavid dynasty, magnificent mosques, palaces, and bridges.

We had tea under the arches of the Si-o-seh Pol (Bridge of Thirty-Three Arches) and then visited the gravesite of Arthur Upham Pope, along the banks of the Ziandeh Rud. The inscription read: "Arthur Upham Pope, American Expert on Persian Art." Pope became deeply involved in the world of Iranian antiquities from the 1920s, and the last shah had arranged for the impoverished American and his wife to be buried here. The enclosure was locked, and the Cultural Heritage Organization held the key, so we could not go in for a closer look.

I experienced my only hostile encounter of the whole trip while crossing one of the crowded bridges. A young man purposely slapped my chest as we passed each other. Instinctively, I yelled after him with a string of expletives I had learned in Tuyserkan. That must have taken him by surprise.

More typical were the two young women who came up to us and wanted to speak English, which was their major at a nearby university. Men stared, but the two women did not seem to mind. Then a woman with her husband conversed with us, saying that she had a daughter in Vancouver with whom she had recently spent a year. Later, a family from Mashhad, two boys and their father, stopped to talk. One son asked us what we thought of George Bush. We chatted a while then parted with smiles and handshakes all around.

A lot of restoration work was being done on the old monuments, and it appeared to be of high quality. The former Shah Mosque had been renamed Imam Mosque. It appeared even more beautiful than I remembered. Fortunately, none of these structures had been damaged in the war.

On our last night we had tea in the garden of the former Shah Abbas Hotel, now named the Abbasi, where we had honeymooned in 1972. It looked much the same. Then, we bought boxes of *gaz* (nougat) as gifts for friends in Tehran. The variety from Isfahan was famous. I could never resist this chewy sweet, although it could be tough on fillings.

As we drove northward, Asghar told us a revealing story about a run-in he had with a Mr. Kaveh, who was a religious leader in Isfahan associated with the Basij. Kaveh had challenged a Dutch tourist over her dress and poked her with his finger. Asghar told him he had no right to interfere with tourists and their guide, whereupon both were taken to the headquarters of local intelligence. Asghar was kept there until 4:00 a.m. and told that he had to apologize to Kaveh before they would let him go. If he did not, the officer remarked, Kaveh would probably set the Basij on him. Asghar did what he had to, but ever since, the two had studiously avoided each other.[10]

I noticed that farmers working in the fields, all wore large straw hats. There were none of those in the 1970s. Then, farmers wore traditional hats, which identified their tribal or ethnic origins

---

[10] A paramilitary volunteer militia now part of the Iranian Revolutionary Guards Corps. The Basij has a presence in almost every Iranian city.

but did not protect them much from the sun. This was definitely an improvement.

We stopped briefly in Natanz, which was much in the news recently, as Iran was said to have a nuclear facility nearby. We saw no sign of that. We did visit the beautiful Friday Mosque with its single minaret and conical dome and much exquisite tile work at the entrance. Inside we found plain white chalk walls and the tomb of a revered Sufi (a mystic) saint. Until recently his followers had lived and worshipped there, but the present government, representing orthodoxy, forced them out.

In Kashan, which we had visited thirty-one years before, we searched for the tomb of one of Iran's most illustrious rulers, Shah Abbas the Great (1587-1628 CE). It was he who had built many of the wonderful monuments in Isfahan, but he lay buried in an unadorned tomb in this small desert city. It was located in a modest building dedicated to a local holy man, who seemed to attract much more attention. The shah's actual tomb chamber was underground, and access had been blocked. On the surface rested a simple black stone coffin with inscription. The shah's name had been scraped away from one end. I assumed the Cultural Heritage Organization wanted to minimize public acclaim for the great Safavid ruler.

Continuing north along the edge of the desert toward Tehran, we were often the only vehicle in sight on the new, six-lane highway. About thirty-five kilometers south of Tehran, we passed the site of the new Imam Khomaini International Airport, which was due to open in 2007. We also could see the golden dome of the mausoleum of Ayatollah Khomaini next to the vast Behesht-e Zahra cemetery, which contained thousands of graves of those who died in the Iran-Iraq War.

We farewelled Asghar at the hotel. He was getting married again on Tuesday, so he would not be driving us to Azerbaijan and Hamadan. He had invited us to his wedding, but we planned to be out of Tehran on that day. He had been a fine driver and companion even if he sometimes became too pushy on the road. We would miss him.

Thinking back on our time in Iran, I was never aware of anyone watching us or keeping check of where we went and whom we saw. We did not always know, ourselves, from day to day what we would be doing. We never submitted a schedule of our activities. Of course, Iran Doostan knew our itinerary when we were traveling outside Tehran. We did wonder from time to time if Asghar had been delegated to keep an eye on us, but he never gave us any reason to think that was the case. If he was undercover, he was incredibly good at it. It might have helped that we had an official invitation from Tehran University. And then, too, this was the time of President Khatami, when a new openness was present in the land. I thought, also, that we were not important enough to be spied on. Perhaps we were just naïve.

The day after our return was another marathon, as we tried to do all we could in the short time we had left. I am afraid we raced around like stereotypical Americans. We had arranged to have lunch with Sara, whom we had met in Istanbul, and her family. Her father, Jalal, picked us up in his old, battered car. Her brother, Sina, and her mother, Ziba, were waiting for us at their apartment. She had prepared a wonderful lunch and the conversation flowed. Sara was a bit apprehensive because she had not yet received her US visa, and also, I think, because she was concerned at the prospect of being so far away from her parents if her visa did arrive.

Jalal, who had a PhD in physics, had worked at Shiraz University and at Tehran Polytechnic, but he was now working for a private company that made lighting. He was their director of research and development. He never mentioned why he had left the academic world.

He was a cynic, as were many Iranians, even young ones, I discovered. He also believed avidly in conspiracies even though he was so well educated. This was a national characteristic I remembered well from my Peace Corps days; it may have become even more pronounced since the revolution.

During our travels, we were told repeatedly that the United States had orchestrated the overthrow of the shah, that the French had conspired to return Khomaini to Iran, and on and on. It was almost impossible to disabuse someone of this belief. Accepting this conspiracy theory removed any sense of agency from the people. If a particular venture succeeded, it was due to some great foreign plot; if it failed, the same.

I am happy to say that Sara did eventually receive her visa and in time earned her graduate degree from WMU. We visited her often and when her parents came to see her, we extended our hospitality to them in Grand Haven. Later, Sara accepted a good job in California, and her parents settled there as well.

That evening we were entertained again at Mr. Ehsani's apartment. This time the whole extended family had gathered for the occasion. They were about thirty strong. The hosts had outdone themselves in preparing the meal. I am sure Mahvash had a lot of help in the kitchen. Bashiri came from Kermanshah for the occasion. We talked and talked about the good times in Tuyserkan, remembering especially Terry O'Donnell and Rick Sullivan, both of whom had recently passed away.

All the young women in the family had college degrees and worked outside the home. The family members seemed to be even more tightly connected with each other and dependent on each other than before the revolution. Putting decorum briefly aside, Nasrollah's widow when she saw me blurted out, "You've gotten so old!" Strangely, her comment made me feel like I belonged, for she never would have said that to an outsider. Teimour had recently made the pilgrimage to Mecca; he had always seemed the most religious of the four Ehsani brothers. Mr. Ehsani, who had experienced considerable illness, confided to me that he had doubts about an afterlife. I, an agnostic, tried to reassure him. We left sometime after midnight, knowing that no one would leave until we did.

The next day was a religious holiday. The city was reasonably quiet, so we decided to try to find the house in Tajrish where Ginny had lived in 1971. We wandered the streets, whose names had all been changed since the revolution. Not only that but tall apartment buildings covered the blocks that had formerly contained private homes. Nothing looked familiar. We asked many times. People would either say they did not know that address, or they would unintentionally send us on a wild goose chase. We were about to give up, when a man in a local shop told me exactly where the street could be found. And he was right. When we arrived, we were surprised to see that the beautiful home built in the late 1960s was being pulled down to make way for another high-rise. Rubble filled the pool in the backyard, where Ginny had once sunned herself. Only the spiral staircase, on which we had stood for our wedding photos, was still intact. If we had arrived a few days later all traces would have disappeared. As we left, we took a souvenir ceramic tile from a nearby debris pile.[11]

The next morning, I set out in a taxi to find the new Ganjineh Asnad (National Archives) building in North Tehran. I used taxis a lot while we were in Tehran, and I never had any disagreement over fares. I liked to listen to the drivers' stories, often tales of woe. On

---

[11] The Halls were saddened to learn the fate of their lovely home.

one particular day the driver told me his sad story how he had been dismissed from the military in the early days of the revolution. Apparently, he had been struggling ever since to care for his family. As we passed one of the large billboards erected by the regime to feature leading religious figures, the driver shook his fist at them, saying "they are the ones responsible for all this misfortune!" All this as he sped along at high speed in heavy traffic.[12]

I discovered that many drivers did not know their way around the burgeoning city, and we had no GPS then. Sometimes, I could direct the driver, sometimes we just wandered. My search for the archive was a wandering day. We had little success finding the building until we asked a new passenger. She told us immediately. To get there the driver backed down the one-way street against on-coming traffic until he reached the entrance to the expressway, and off we went. We soon spied the complex, but we were on the wrong side of the busy highway. The driver stopped at the side of the road and suggested I cross the eight lanes of traffic on foot. Remarkably, I did just that.

Once I arrived safely on the other side, I made my way to the new building complex. It had not officially opened yet, but one of the librarians I had met earlier suggested I contact Dr. K. Kiani at the center for documents. Usually, one must have made prior arrangements to get an appointment, but I was lucky. The guard kept my passport at the entrance and showed me to the deputy director's office. We had tea and much talk. There was the obligatory lecture about the evil ways of the American government that was trying to dominate the world. Then we got down to business. He presented me with a book full of documents from the archive relating to foreign archaeological expeditions in the interwar years. The editor was Marzieh Yazdani, who, unfortunately, was then in Paris, completing her doctorate. While I was with him, I mentioned that I had an invitation from Dr. Reza Nezar-Ahari at the Foreign Ministry Archive. He knew him well and telephoned him, allowing me to set up a meeting there as well. Then, he took me on a tour of the building, which was very impressive. I was not allowed to take photos, but he showed off their state-of-the-art storage facility. We parted warmly.

---

[12] In addition to religious leaders, these billboards might portray deeds of heroic sacrifice that took place during the Iran-Iraq War or of acts of resistance to the Great Satan, that is, the United States.

At the diplomatic archive, the director was very welcoming, telling me briefly the history of the institution, where all the records of the foreign office were stored. These extended back to the reign of Fath Ali Shah (1797-1834 CE). He showed me a document signed by Napoleon and the gold-cloth cover of the Treaty of Turk-menchay (1828 CE) with its elaborate Russian seal. Documents had been typed pretty consistently from the beginning of Reza Shah's reign in the mid-1920s, thus, researchers of the Pahlavi dynasty would not have to struggle with handwritten sources. The director said that most materials up to the revolution were available for research. He also handed me four volumes of published documents from their archive on American, British, French, and German archaeological expeditions in Iran, 1899-1940. He assured me that they represented everything in the archive on the subject. It seemed as though I could easily have done my own research then and there, but that was not my mission.

Actually, I had come to Iran to visit archaeological sites, unaware that I would leave with a mass of new primary sources. I thought I had almost finished writing, now I would need to translate the relevant documents in the five books and incorporate any new material into the existing manuscript. That would take time. This proved, of course, a welcome bonus from the trip. Later, when I cross-checked the information in the volumes, it did not appear that any important material had been withheld.

For years, I had been told by more senior scholars that one should not pay much attention to Iranian archives because they were totally disorganized and held little of interest. I remember a disparaging picture one author constructed of boxes of open documents sitting near a raised window in one repository. When the wind blew, he wrote, several documents fluttered to the floor. A janitor wandered by, picked up the papers and stuck them in the nearest box, which may or may not have been where they came from.

Now, I had seen with my own eyes, that such dismissive anecdotes presented a false picture. The Iranian government archives were well organized and contained a vast array of important historical material. This was certainly, for me, one of the more important conclusions of the trip.

Finally, the day of my presentation arrived. I had been invited to discuss my project at the Center for Dialogue Among Civilizations, an institution set up under the auspices of President Khatami. The audience was made up of social scientists. I had prepared either to read my paper or summarize it, whichever seemed more appropriate, but certainly in English. What I quickly observed was that most of the audience did not speak English. My host for the evening, Dr. Azadi, the dean of social sciences at Tehran University, asked me to summarize my work in Persian. With some trepidation, I obliged. I am not sure what sense the members of the audience made of my limited vocabulary, but their perceptive questions indicated that they had understood some of what I intended. I had good conversations with several graduate students afterwards and during the formal dinner that was held in our honor at the President's Club in Elahieh. That was my only formal obligation during the visit.

Regarding the use of English, I had noticed that wherever we went in Iran fewer people seemed to know the language. Before the revolution students studied it from junior high school, but that was not the case now. Then, too, almost no English-speaking tourists visited the country. One benefit of all this change was that we no longer had children on the street yelling, "Hello Meester!" at us as they had frequently done in the 1970s. The downside was that graduate students, for example, often struggled to comprehend scholarly literature in English. Even with my Iranian friends, basic conversations in English were now rare.

We set off on our second road trip to the north and west on August 5. Our new driver was no Asghar. He could be surly at times. Worse than that, his air conditioner did not work properly, so he tried to convince us that the air outside was so cool we did not need it.

At least I persuaded him to take us to Musaddiq's village and gravesite on our way to Sultanieh and Zanjan. When we had first arrived in Tehran, I had hired a taxi to take us to Ahmadabad, the village where Musaddiq had spent his last years under house arrest. The driver clearly did not know its location; I was not even certain he knew who Musaddiq was. We asked country folk along the way but got little help. Eventually we got to Ahmadabad, the wrong one. It turned out there were many villages in the area with that name. So, we returned to the hotel late that afternoon disappointed and despairing of ever being able to complete our pilgrimage.

Now, we were headed to Ahmadabad-e Mostowfi, and I was delighted. We saw no signs or any indication along the way that the former prime minister lay buried here—under his kitchen floor. We had no problem gaining entrance to the compound. Apparently, few visitors made their way to the site; the museum was empty, and the garden neglected. The only decoration in the modest home were faded posters of the members of Musaddiq's cabinet lining the kitchen walls. I was thrilled to be standing at last at the great patriot's final resting place. The government surely hoped that he would be forgotten in this the fiftieth year after his overthrow.

I reflected for a moment on Musaddiq's place in history. Both the shah and his successors had tried, without much success, to diminish the stature of the man in the eyes of his countrymen. Numerous scholars had spent countless hours trying to understand him and interpret his actions. And after all that, he still remained something of an enigma. I think he would have heartily approved of all the attention.

In late afternoon, we arrived at Sultanieh, the site of the tomb of Oljeitu (1304-1316 CE), the Ilkhanid ruler. This was one of four archaeological sites on which the government had decided to spend considerable sums. The others were Chogha Zanbil, Persepolis and Isfahan, appropriately, two pre-Islamic and two Islamic sites.

Archaeology had come under a cloud in the early revolutionary years. Practitioners of this discipline had become too closely identified with the Pahlavi dynasty and its claims to links with the ancient glory of pre-Islamic Iran. Visits to the early sites had been discouraged. The archaeology department at Tehran University had been closed for several years. Now, however, leaders of the Islamic Republic of Iran, beginning with President Ali Akbar Hashemi Rafsanjani, had made their peace with the archaeologists, and they had come to embrace the entire history of the nation.

This tomb complex was stunningly beautiful even though much of it was covered with scaffolding inside and out. We had a chance to visit the small ceramics factory on the site where replacement tiles for the structure were being made. No accurate formulas for the original glazes remained, so the chemist had to make thousands of test tiles to get the exact colors. The work was very sophisticated. Some American scholars had come the previous year to provide restoration advice. Sultanieh was now a World Heritage Site.

We had never visited the city of Zanjan. We spent a pleasant evening there, where we met two students, who studied English at a branch of the Islamic Azad University in nearby Takestan. They practiced their English very earnestly with us for an hour or so.

The countryside of Zanjan and Western Azerbaijan that we drove through the following day was beautiful. The harvest was underway, and we saw golden fields of wheat everywhere. Rooftops of village houses were piled high with bundles of clover and alfalfa for animal feed in winter.

Our next stop, Takht-e Suleyman, a Sasanian (224-651 CE) and Ilkhanid (1256-1335 CE) location, had just been designated a World Heritage Site. We wandered in and out of buildings with decorative, vaulted ceilings, arches, and doorways. A deep, volcanic lake lay nearby. The Germans had excavated here in earlier times, and they had left a narrow-gauge railway that was being removed. We talked to two young Iranian archaeologists, who spent about two months here each year. They seemed to know a great deal about previous excavations at the site.

We set out at midday for Hamadan, last stop on our trip, and arrived in late afternoon. As in Isfahan, we did not recognize the modern city. It had grown so much. We stayed at the Hotel Bu Ali, the same place I had lived for three months in 1971 when doing training for Peace Corps. There were few other guests.

We met old friends, Esmaeil Momtaz and his wife Mina, in the garden and had dinner together. Esmaeil was a ten-year old boy when I arrived in Tuyserkan in 1968. He now taught English at the university in Hamadan. His wife was an even younger girl then. She had become a midwife. They were relatives of Mr. Ehsani and Mr. Bashiri. They now had two children; their daughter Niloufar had come with them to meet us. After dinner they drove us up to Ganj-Nameh for a view over the city at night. Mina told us that a friend of hers had had a nightmare recently in which the United States attacked Iran. Perhaps this was common in the months following the American invasion of nearby Iraq.

We talked to the Bashiris on Esmaeil's cellphone. They urged us to visit them in Kermanshah, but we could not. Esmaeil told me that his family in Malayer had moved out to the villages during the war with Iraq to avoid the missiles. Several friends who stayed in the city had perished. It was almost midnight when we said goodbye.

We have remained in contact with Esmaeil and Mina, who have lived in Scotland for many years. He studied for and received his doctorate in applied linguistics, and he now teaches English to foreign students at the university in Aberdeen.

The next day we visited Lolejin, the pottery village of Hamadan. When I first went there in 1968 (and with Ginny in 1971), it lay a kilometer or so beyond the edge of the city, but now the city had spread out and enveloped it. We spent a long time examining a porcelain and a clay factory, including their kilns. Ginny, who studies ceramics, was in her element. They told us they exported their wares throughout the Middle East and Europe. They especially marketed to Iraq. I questioned Hussein, a potter, about this, as the war was then on-going. How would they cross the border, I asked? He told me that people and goods continued to cross in both directions all the time. You just had to know the right places. I gave him a GVSU pen as a *yadigari* (souvenir). He was touched.

This was the closest we would come to Tuyserkan in our travels. It lay on the other side of the mountains from Hamadan. I had decided not to return to my Peace Corps site because most of my friends had by then either died or left for Tehran. For them as for me, Tuyserkan was a fading memory.

The city, I was told, had changed almost beyond recognition. It was no longer the small, isolated settlement of the early 1970s. Since my last brief visit there in September 1973, the population had more than tripled to over fifty thousand. The roads into the valley were asphalted long ago, making access in all seasons easier. Kuchehs had been widened and turned into proper roads. The government had built a dam above Gazandar Bala, where the water flow could be regulated year-round. The tomb of Habakkuk that used to sit somewhat neglected in an open wheat-field, now lay at the center of a fine plaza. Symbolic of the changes, there was now a branch of Islamic Azad University in the city. Later, Tuyserkan would gain some brief notoriety in the protests of 2018, when police responded with deadly force, killing six individuals.

On the road back to Tehran, we stopped briefly along the river below Avaj Pass to take pictures of a shepherd, his flock, and his dogs. In the grand Iranian tradition, he invited us to be his guests and to join him and his friend for tea and lunch. We thanked him heartily, explaining that we had to be in Tehran by late afternoon.

Everywhere along the road were speed bumps. This was a new addition. For some unknown reason, Reza referred to them as "sandwiches." He insisted on taking the back roads rather than the highway, saying it was more scenic. I suspected he had other reasons. Anyway, he got us back at the promised hour of 5:00 p.m., and that was the last we saw of him.

Incredibly, we had been invited to yet a third gathering at Mr. Ehsani's that same evening, so we had to hurry. Even more people had gathered to say farewell. Again, much good conversation, good memories, excellent food. I remember someone told a disturbing story about twenty Tuyserkan policemen, who had been put to death in grizzly fashion early in the revolution. I assumed they were suspected of supporting the old regime. Once again, we did not climb into our taxi until late in the evening.

The last day in Iran had arrived, and we still had several tasks to complete. We went back to St. Abraham's, where we had married in 1972. We met two priests, one from Pakistan and the other from Ireland. Their Dominican order had a long history in Iran, going back to the late 13th century and the time of the IlKhanids. They had a difficult time right after the revolution. They were expelled for a while but then allowed to return. Maids from the Philippines made up most of their congregation in 2003. They told us that Father O'Farrell still came back now and again from Dublin.

One more stop before we left. We went to the nearby Atlas Hotel (formerly the Atlantic) for a late lunch, which was excellent. The garden had changed surprisingly little since our first meeting there in 1971. We vowed that when we returned, we would stay there.

I had agreed to interviews with reporters from two major newspapers, *Iran* and *Hamshahri*. The fiftieth anniversary of Musaddiq's overthrow was only a few days away, and they wanted to ask me questions about him. They knew that I had written a great deal about the former Iranian prime minister. They asked penetrating questions, and the interviews went on far longer than I had expected. It seemed as if they wanted to blame Musaddiq for his own overthrow. Fortunately, Hadi had agreed to be present and to translate carefully what I said. The interviews would be published on 28 Mordad (August 19), the day of the coup d'etat in 1953. No sooner had they departed than the photographer from *Hamshahri* came by to take my picture for the article. (Later, back in the States, I received copies of the articles based on the interviews.)

After the reporters had left, Hadi expressed some of his own thoughts about recent political events. He said that Ayatollah Khomaini had been a great liberal leader, but his message had been drowned out by the clerics of Qom. His generation, he told me, loved Khomaini. The revolution did much for the people of Iran, especially in the villages and small towns, for the shah had focused only on the large cities. Rural areas obtained better drinking water, good roads, and electricity. He had worked for the new government doing surveys in the southeast of the country and found villages where there were hardly any signs of the twentieth century. I must admit, this surprised me, for Tuyserkan and many of its villages had clean water, electricity, and schools when I arrived in 1968. In hindsight, it appeared that there had been major disparities among the various regions of the country.

We said goodbye to Hadi, thanking him for all he had done to make our visit more pleasant. We knew we would see him again, for he traveled abroad frequently and often visited Tom Gordon in Michigan.

I should explain that soon after moving to Michigan, we had reestablished ties with Tom, who lived in the Upper Peninsula. We visited him at least once a year while camping on Lake Superior. Tom had stayed in Iran right up to the revolution and flew out on one of the last planes in early 1979. He then taught English in Saudi Arabia and Kuwait. He was taken captive by the Iraqi forces in Kuwait City in August 1990, spending four months as a hostage in Mosul. Saddam Hussein released him and the other hostages in early December. Tom then taught again in Saudi Arabia for several years before retiring and coming home.

On our last evening in Tehran, Professor Tavasoli came to say goodbye, and we talked for an hour or so. He told me that he belonged to the party of the late Mehdi Bazargan, the Freedom Movement of Iran, which was now headed by Dr. Yazdi. In 2001 they were all rounded up and put in prison. He had only spent a few days there, but others were still waiting to stand trial. The party was forbidden to put up candidates for parliament. He had served earlier as chancellor of Isfahan University and dean of the social sciences at Tehran University, but he had been removed from his post and returned to teaching. He could have gone extremely far, he said, if he had accepted the current policies. I thanked him for his assistance during our stay.

We had booked a late-night departure for Istanbul, so we got into bed at 10:30 p.m. to try to sleep for a few hours. Then the phone rang. It was Ehsani and Mahvash calling to say goodbye and to wish us safe travels. We chatted for a few minutes, not knowing that would be our last conversation with Mr. Ehsani. (He died on December 17, 2013.) What a remarkable friendship; what a privilege to have known them both.

Asghar came right on time at 2:00 a.m. to take us to the airport. He was full of bustle. The city slept, but the airport was wide awake. He had to park the car a long distance from the terminal, and we trundled the luggage along the road, weaving in and out of traffic. Once the Turkish Airlines counter opened, we sadly said goodbye to Asghar—he was one of the precious finds of our trip.

And so, we bid farewell to Iran. The visit had proven more successful than we could have hoped. Our love for Iran continued. I was already developing plans for the future.

Indissoluble Ties

Istanbul seemed worlds away from Tehran. Whereas we had seen very few foreign tourists in Iran, and no Americans, visitors now filled this city. They came mostly from Spain, Italy and Germany, but we met some fellow countrymen as well. We spent the next two days soaking up the relaxed atmosphere along the Bosphorus, climbing the walls of Rumeli Hisar, strolling the delightful grounds of the Blue Mosque and Topkapi Palace. And then we took off for the States and return to the quiet of West Michigan.

Not long after we got back, I received a call from someone at the US State Department inquiring about our recent trip to Iran. I learned later that the department contributed funds to the AIIS, even while discouraging travel there. I suggested that it would really help bilateral exchange if the department would modify its travel warning, which was quite unwarranted. The Iranians were exceedingly friendly wherever we went. He thanked me for my views.

I was so energized by the positive reception we had received in Iran that I returned to campus with a well-thought-out plan for the coming year. I would offer to teach a special course on the history of Iran in the winter semester. During the spring break, I would return to Iran with any of the students who wanted to make the trip. We would be gone for two weeks.

While in Iran I had asked the travel company if they could organize such a visit, and they said yes. Tehran University officials had also shown interest in hosting us. This might just be the first big breakthrough in bilateral relations. We might become pioneers like the American table tennis team that had visited China in April 1971, initiating so-called "ping-pong diplomacy."

I ran with this plan for several months, like a fish with a baited hook in its mouth, and then someone in the administration set the hook. One day I received an e-mail asking me to visit the university lawyer as soon as possible. In the discussion that followed, he told me that if the university allowed our group to go to Iran, its insurer, AIG, would cancel all the university's coverage. Clearly, this would be unacceptable, so we could not go.

I was devastated. Although I was almost sixty years old, one might say I was still too naïve and much too idealistic or perhaps, unrealistic. I did teach the special course that winter, but there was no trip to Iran. More than likely, parents would have stopped us if the university had not. Still, there are moments when I dream of what might have been.

On a more positive note, we were able to hire a new colleague, Chad Lingwood, who happened to be a specialist in medieval Iranian history. It comforted me to know that even after my retirement, our students would continue to study the wonders of Iran's past. Perhaps, one day, Chad would get the opportunity to take GVSU students on that long-delayed journey to Tehran.

In August 2011, I received an e-mail from Hamed Bashiri, who was born long after we had left Iran in 1973. I had never met him, although I knew from Esmaeil that he was living in Montreal and studying for his doctorate. To my great delight, he told me that his parents were with him at the moment, and his father wanted to talk with me. Would I, please, call them.

This was wonderful news. I called, we reminisced, and I was soon on my way to Montreal for a grand reunion over Labor Day Weekend. Ginny was away in Australia, so I travelled alone.

When we met again, it seemed as if no great time had intervened. Ghassem and I picked up where we had left off. We went for long walks in the park, and one day we all drove north to a special resort Hamed knew. Ashraf now wore hijab, which surprised me somewhat. She had also made the pilgrimage to Mecca. Ghassem's views about religion had not changed as far as I could tell, and he teased her a bit, but it was all good natured. I recalled that Mahvash had also become more outwardly religious when we visited in 2003. She had kept her head covered at home, even while insisting that Ginny remove her scarf and her long coat.

I enjoyed meeting Hamed for the first time. A fine young man, who did everything he could to make his parents and this temporary guest, comfortable. (I was staying at a nearby hotel.) His mother cooked wonderful dishes while I was there. She used many ingredients they had brought with them from Iran. All too soon, I had to return to Michigan, not knowing when or even if we would see each other again. Nevertheless, we had been fortunate to enjoy these few special days together.[13]

In 2012 the Iranian Studies Association decided to hold its bi-annual conference in Istanbul. It was thought that this would allow Iranian scholars, who did not need visas for Turkey, to attend the conference and interact with their American and European counter-parts. There was much excitement and expectation. Unfortunately, a short time before the gathering, a leading Iranian cleric announced that the conference was the work of sinister American forces and that any scholar who attended would be lending them support. This had such a chilling effect that not a single Iranian appeared.

The barriers to cross-cultural exchange and understanding seem at times insurmountable. This is not to say that there are no legitimate differences between our two countries, but these have been consistently exaggerated on both sides for political purposes.

With every passing year, fewer and fewer Americans can claim any firsthand experience in Iran. Any individual who can is becoming, as John Limbert once jokingly remarked, "an Iranosaurus." Limbert had been appointed U.S. Deputy Assistant Secretary of State for Iran in 2009, but he resigned in frustration less than a year later. Many of his colleagues came to view him as too much of an Iranophile. The danger becomes that with no personal experience in the country, policy makers can more easily believe the worst of Iran and Iranians. They become the Other, just as the Chinese Communists did in the 1950s and 1960s.

On a brighter note, the Peace Corps Iran Association does what it can to inform the American public about Iran. The PCIA came into existence a decade ago following the first reunion of PCV's who had served in Iran, 1962-1976. In Portland, Oregon, Terry O'Donnell's hometown, we celebrated the 50th anniversary of the founding of the Peace Corps. Approximately three hundred former volunteers attended the gathering in early August 2011. (The exact number of Iran PCVs is unknown, but the estimate is around eighteen hundred individuals.) A survey indicated that many former volunteers welcomed the idea of having a formal association. A few stalwarts pursued the idea and turned it into a reality. Since that first meeting there have been four others, Boston 2013, Austin 2015, Annapolis 2017, and San Diego 2019.

---

[13] They were scheduled to return to Montreal in summer 2020 but had to cancel due to the pandemic.

Will there be another one? The membership is aging. The
Peace Corps left Iran in 1976, after a vote by the then-Volunteers.
Apparently, the majority believed that the Iranian government had
enough resources of its own, and Peace Corps Volunteers could be
used more effectively elsewhere. Therefore, the youngest member
of PCIA, today, should be at least sixty-five years old, perhaps older.

Nevertheless, active members have established educational and
outreach activities, an advocacy committee, an online book discussion group, historical archives of the Peace Corps in Iran, and two
informative newsletters. Hopefully, these activities will continue
long into the future. But we have to wonder whether any of us will
be around when friendly bilateral relations are finally restored.

The desire to preserve collective memories of Iran before the
revolution, has spread well beyond American Peace Corps Volunteers. Alumni of Alam High School, for example, have been con-
tinually active in preserving the history of that unique experiment in
education. Due to their success, Alam will be remembered well into
the future.

A number of former students organized the publication of a
book, *Alam High School* (2018), detailing their varied experiences
at the Mashhad high school in the years, 1975-1979. This has been
supplemented with video clips, which are available on You Tube.

Two   Iranian-American   filmmakers,   Saman   Yaghmai-
Aledavoud and Houtan Yaghmai, set out on their own to make a
documentary of Alam High School. They raised funds and traveled
around the country interviewing former students and faculty in
2014. The crew spent three days with us in late October of that year
filming. In addition to interviews, they also filmed in one of my
classes, in which I talked with the students about my experiences in
Iran. I told them that I still peruse newspapers and journals starting
at the back, as I would any Persian publication. The visit proved a
great success. After much editing they finally finished the film in
2017. From them I first learned that several Alam alumni had been
imprisoned at the former school after the revolution.[14]

One of the unexpected and most welcome outcomes of this
process was the fact that it brought us together with Hamid and Ma-

---

[14] Over the years, I often met one-on-one with Grand Valley students, who
were interested in joining the Peace Corps, to talk about my own experiences.

hin Ekbia. Hamid is an alumnus of the school and currently a faculty member at Indiana University, my alma mater. Although he was not in any of my classes at Alam, we share memories of those years. The four of us have enjoyed some happy times together since the making of the film.

Mount Ararat seen from just inside Turkish border on road to Erzurum,
September 1973

Ginny and Asghar (to her immediate left), talking with girls whose fathers had
died in Iran-Iraq War, Imam Mosque, Isfahan, summer 2003

Ehsani and Mahvash with grandson, Farhad, and Author at their
Tehran home, 2003

Gathering of twelve Alam alumni, with Hadi Navid sitting between us,
Tehran, 2003

Asghar, our driver, relaxing with village couple in Bishapur, 2003

Skeletal remains of staircase in Australian ambassador's former
home, Tehran, 2003 (Compare to wedding photo, 1972)

Haystacks on village roofs, near Zanjan, August 2003

Potter in kiln full of porcelain vases and
teapots at Lolejin outside Hamadan,
August 2003

Ginny and Jim at St. Abraham's where they were married thirty-one years earlier, Tehran, 2003

Ghassem, Ashraf, and Hamed Bashiri (l. to r.), Montreal, September 2011

Epilogue

And thus, at the end of all these recollections and after more than two years of preparation, we arrived at the night of the grand opening of the exhibition, September 18, 2017. We had stayed away from the gallery during the long period of installing the objects. We had anticipated a larger role in deciding how the items would be arranged, but we were only consulted from time to time when the staff needed more information. Occasionally, we got a glimpse of different pieces of the exhibition, but we had little idea what the whole might look like.

Then, the day before the opening, we were invited to a private viewing. I am sure the members of the staff were as nervous as we were. We need not have worried. The exhibition was amazing. Everything had been tastefully displayed to make the greatest impact. Items had been clustered in ways we probably would not have chosen, but the effect was superior to anything we could have conceived. We could readily appreciate the skill of the professionals. And even the humblest of artifacts took on a new luster once placed behind the glass of the cases or hung on the walls with proper lighting. We were thrilled. Although we had lived with these items for decades, we now saw them with new eyes.

What made the whole affair so interesting, we thought, was the fact that each item on display had its own story, and we were able to provide that information to those who had done the installation. Pride of place went to the Baluchi carpet that Ahmad had purchased for us. Then, there was the copper candleholder from our honeymoon in Isfahan, the Qibla indicator that Terry had willed to us, an abacus similar to Manuchehr's, the Russian brass samovar from the Hamadan bazaar, and much more. Each had a tale to tell.

The opening reception had been organized with great care. The crowd of attendees almost overwhelmed us. Everyone had questions about this or that item or group of items. Matthew, his partner, Jeffrey, and Zachary came, along with old friends from Iran, Tom Gordon and Jim and Mary King. Members of the university turned out in large numbers as did many students. After two hours, a time that went by in a flash, we proceeded to a wonderful Middle Eastern banquet hosted by the president of the university. We used that occasion to thank the gallery staff for all their efforts in making the exhibition such a success.[1]

Over the following weeks we were kept enjoyably busy. We made a half-dozen informal presentations. We arranged our first meeting with Hamid and Mahin Ekbia, with whom we were able to tour the gallery. We used those weeks to talk with the gallery representatives about donating artifacts to the university's collection. We realized that we had far too many items for our much smaller home in California, and we knew that what we left behind would be well cared for and available always to the members of the university community. In spite of some second thoughts on our part, we finally agreed to donate a representative selection of objects from our collection.

The exhibition was extended into early November. Then, suddenly, it was over. What a wonderful experience, we thought; what a satisfying way to end our day-to-day relationship with Grand Valley. Certainly, we would continue our interest in Iran and the Middle East as well as our advocacy for improved bilateral relations, although probably with less intensity than in earlier years. Overall, we felt privileged to have shared such a long and rewarding journey.

---

[1] See clip of opening on You Tube,
https://www.youtube.com/watch?v=FFxbineD8Hs

Index